Contents

KEY

71–74
71–74   cross-reference between playscript and teaching resources.

H   in resources = activity suitable for homework.

Introduction

This book contains 4 extracts from plays written and first performed in different countries from around the world. Thousands of miles separate these plays but a similar theme runs through each of them. Each of the plays is concerned with relationships between parents and children:

- *The Government Inspector*, a classic Russian comedy, shows the bizarre relationship between a mother and daughter when they are flattered by the attentions of a con man who is posing as a Government official
- *Summer of the Aliens* from Australia explores what happens when a 14 year old boy's father returns after 3 years' unexplained absence
- *Anowa* examines the point in a young girl's life in Ghana when she leaves home to marry the man she loves much against the wishes of her mother
- *Loon Boy* is about an 11 year old boy who has been in and out of foster homes and has had little or no relationship with his parents. In place of a father or mother, a special relationship develops with a Foster Carer who also looks after wild birds on a lake in Canada.

This selection of plays and resources is suitable for study, exploration and/or performance within the GCSE Drama specifications offered by AQA, Edexcel, OCR and WJEC. The extracts have been edited so that they form a coherent whole and can be used for the performance component of any GCSE Drama course.

Each extract lasts between fifteen and twenty minutes.

Play 1 requires a cast of 2 females and 2 males (plus non-speaking extras)

Play 2 requires a cast of 1 female and 3 males

Play 3 requires a cast of 2 females and 1 male

Play 4 requires a cast of 2 females and 1 male (the male role can be changed to a female role) plus puppeteers or dancers.

An outline of the GCSE Drama examination specifications can be found at the end of this introduction. A number and letter, for example 4d, identifies each resource activity and this is referenced against the appropriate learning and teaching objectives from the two major GCSE Drama specifications.

This particular collection of plays also fulfils the National Curriculum Programme of study for English requirement at Key Stages 3 and 4 for pupils to be introduced to texts from different cultures and traditions. Each extract offers a range of opportunities for practical drama work, discussion, reading and written work. A chart matches each extract's

Duty and Lies

Comparing Times and Cultures

Play selection and
resource material by

Steve Lewis

Series Consultant
Steve Cockett

Cricklade College LRS

Published by Collins Educational, an imprint of HarperCollins*Publishers* Ltd,
77–85 Fulham Palace Road, London W6 8JB

www.**Collins**Education.com
On-line support for schools and colleges

© Selection and Activities copyright Steve Lewis 2002

First published 2002

ISBN 000 713142 9

British Library Cataloguing in Publication Data
A catalogue record for this book is available from the British Library.

Commissioned by Isabelle Zahar, edited by Mark Dudgeon, picture research by Sarah McNaught and Mark Dudgeon.

Design by Jordan Publishing Design, cover design by Jordan Publishing Design, cover photograph of *The Government Inspector* courtesy of Zoë Dominic.

Acknowledgements
The following permissions to reproduce material are gratefully acknowledged:
Photographs: Zoë Dominic, p.24; Brisbane Arts theatre, p56; Charlotte Thege/Images of African Photobank, p77; Corbis, p107.
Text and Extracts: *The Government Inspector* – Nikolai Gogol translated by Edward O. March & Jeremy Brooks, Eyre Methuen Publishing Ltd; *Summer of the Aliens* – Louis Nowra, Currency Press, Sydney, 1992; *Anowa* from *Contemporary African Plays*, Methuen Publishing Ltd; *Loon Boy* – Kathleen McDonnell, Playwrights Canada Press, 1998; AQA Specifications are reproduced by permission of the Assessment and Qualifications Alliance, p.3; 'Do a Dance for Daddy' from *Invade My Privacy*, Jonathan Cape, London, 1978, p122; 'Being There' from *No Holds Barred: The Raving Beauties Choose New Poems by Women*, Women's Press Ltd. 1985, p123.

Every effort has been made to trace copyright holders, but in some cases this has proved impossible. The publishers would be happy to hear from any copyright holder that has not been acknowledged.

Production by Katie Morris, printed and bound in Thailand by Imago

For amateur or professional productions of *Loon Boy*, please contact: Playwrights Union of Canada, 54 Wolseley Street, Toronto, Ontario M5T 1A5 – info@puc.ca

You might also like to visit
www.**fire**and**water**.co.uk
The book lover's website

activities to the English Framework, highlighting the main objectives covered.

AQA DRAMA COURSEWORK COVERAGE CHART

Candidates of the AQA Drama GCSE course must offer **two** different options for coursework, one from the list of Scripted Work options and one from the list of Unscripted Work options. At least one of these must be a performance option. Where a technical and design skill option is undertaken it must contribute to a group performance. Each option is divided into three parts, with each part testing a different Assessment Objective (AO):

1 **Response to plays and other types of drama**, in which candidates' ability to *"respond with knowledge and understanding to plays and other types of drama from a performance perspective and to explore relationships and comparisons between texts and dramatic styles of different periods and of different cultures in order to show an awareness of their social context and genre"* is assessed (AO2);

2 **Work in progress**, in which candidates' ability to *"analyse and evaluate the effectiveness of their own and others' work with sensitivity as they develop and present their work in an appropriate format for communication"* is assessed (AO3);

3 **Final presentation (either performance or demonstration/artefact(s))**, in which candidates' ability to *"demonstrate ability in and knowledge and understanding of the practical skills in drama necessary for the realisation of a presentation to an audience, working constructively with others"* is assessed (AO1) (AQA).

AQA Coursework Option	1. The Government Inspector	2. Summer of the Aliens	3. Anowa	4. Loon Boy	Comparing the Four Extracts
Option 1: Devised thematic work		2d; 2g; 2j	3d; 3e; 3j; 3k; 3l; 3m	4e; 4f; 4g; 4k; 4j; 4m	5b; 5d; 5e; 5g
Option 2: Acting	1d; 1e; 1f; 1g; 1h; 1i; 1l	2e; 2g; 2i	3b; 3d; 3e; 3f;	4i; 4l	5c
Option 6: Set	p22–3	p49–50		4a; p105–106	
Option 7: Costume	p23–4	p51	p76–77	p108	
Option 8: Make-up					
Option 9: Properties			3a	4b; p106–107	
Option 10: Masks	*		*	*	
Option 11: Puppets				p107	
Option 12: Lighting		p50	p76	p108	
Option 13: Sound		p51–53; 2b	p108	p108	5a
Option 14: Stage Management	•	•	•	•	

* Masks could be used in these plays   • All these plays can be used as stage management texts

EDEXCEL DRAMA COURSEWORK COVERAGE CHART

The chart below highlights which activities and pages provide opportunities or guidance for work on the different components of Edexcel Paper 1 Unit 1: Drama Exploration. In the workshop for this paper, to be based around at least 2 different types of drama texts, candidates are required to use at least 4 of the explorative strategies (a), at least 2 of the skill areas (b), and to select and use appropriately the elements of drama (c) in their responses to the stimulus material.

Edexcel c/w strategies, skills and elements of drama	1. The Government Inspector	2. Summer of the Aliens	3. Anowa	4. Loon Boy Honey	Comparing the four extracts
(a) Explorative Strategies					
Still image	1j	2i		4m	5e
Thought-tracking		2i		4m	
Narrating		2j	3a	4j	
Hot-seating		2e		4l	
Role-play	1f; 1i	2g	3d; 3l	4g	5a; 5b; 5f
Cross-cutting				4e; 4f	
Forum-theatre		2e	3j		
Marking the moment			3a	4m	
(b) The Drama Medium					
Use of costume, masks, make-up	pp23–24	pp51, 76	p87	p108	pp124–5
Sound/music		pp51–53; 2b	pp76–77	p87; p108	5a; pp124–5
Lighting		pp49, 50	p76	pp98, 108	pp124–5
Space/levels	p23	pp49–50	p76	pp105–6; 4a; 4e	
Set and props	pp22, 26	p49; 2a	p76; 90	4a; 4b	p107
Movement, mime, gesture	1j		p77	4c	5c; 5d
Voice	1a; 1e		3b	·	5c; 5d
Spoken language	1b				5d; 5e
(c) The Elements of Drama					
Action/plot/content	1f	2f;	3c; 3e;	4d	5c
Forms	1b; 1f; 1g; 1c	2c; 2g	3e; 3f; 3k		5h
Climax/anticlimax	1j		3b		
Rhythm/pace/tempo		p60		E	
Contrasts	1d				
Characterisation	1d; 1e; 1h	pp58–60		4i	5c
Conventions		p57	p78		pp125–6
Symbols		p57	p76	4b	

ENGLISH FRAMEWORK OBJECTIVES CHART

English Framework Objective	1. The Government Inspector	2. Summer of the Aliens	3. Anowa	4. Loon Boy Honey	Comparing the four extracts
Comment on the authorial perspectives offered in texts on individuals, community and society in texts from different cultures (R6)	1a; 1j	2g; 2l	3d;3g; 3k; 3n	4d; 4e; 4k; 4o	5b; 5c;
Compare the presentation of ideas, values or emotions in related or contrasting texts (R7)	1b; 1j; 4o; 5a	2k; 4o; 5a	3n; 4o; 5a	4o; 5a	5b; 5c; 5d; 5e; 5f; 5h
Analyse the language, form and dramatic impact of scenes and plays by published dramatists (R14)	1e	2f	3g	4l; 4n	5h
Analyse ways in which different cultural contexts and traditions have influenced language and style (R16)	1b	2a; 2h	3c; 3h; 3i;	4o	5b; 5c; 5h
Make telling use of descriptive detail (W11)	1k	2d;2j	3g; 3m	4n; 4j	5a; 5e
Recognise, evaluate and extend the skills and techniques they have developed through drama (S&L11)	1c; 1d; 1g	2d; 2e; 2g; 2i; 2j	3a; 3b; 3d; 3e; 3h; 3k; 3l	4e; 4f; 4g; 4h; 4i; 4l; 4m	5a; 5b; 5c; 5d; 5e; 5f; 5g
Use a range of drama techniques, including work in role, to explore issues, ideas and meanings (S&L12)	1c; 1d; 1g	2d; 2e; 2g; 2i; 2j	3a; 3b; 3d; 3e; 3h; 3k; 3l	4e; 4f; 4g; 4h; 4i; 4l; 4m	5a; 5b; 5c; 5d; 5e; 5f; 5g
Develop and compare different interpretations of scenes or plays by Shakespeare or other dramatists (S&L13)	1e; 1f; 1h		3n		5h
Convey action, character, atmosphere and tension when scripting and performing plays (S&L14)	1c; 1d; 1g	2d; 2e; 2g; 2i; 2j	3a; 3b; 3h; 3m	4e; 4f; 4i; 4m	5g

EXTRACT 1

The Government Inspector

Nikolai Gogol

NIKOLAI GOGOL

Nikolai Vassilyevich Gogol was born in Sorochintsi, Ukraine in 1809. He started writing for periodicals when he was working as a minor government official in St Petersburg at the age of 20. His writing career as a novelist and dramatist flourished after he met the famous Russian writer Alexander Pushkin in 1831. It was in fact Pushkin who suggested the plot of *The Government Inspector* to Gogol because he himself had been mistaken as some kind of government official while staying in Nizhniy Novgorod, a town some 250 miles east of Moscow.

The Government Inspector (*Revizor* in Russian and often translated as *The Inspector General*) was written in 1835 and first performed at the Alexandrinsky Theatre, St Petersburg on April 19th 1836 in the presence of Tsar Nicholas and was an instant success. However, Gogol was sensitive to the criticism of those in authority who considered the play to be subversive and left Russia to travel Europe for much of the rest of his life. He wrote two other complete plays, *Marriage* (written 1835, first performed 1842) and *The Gamblers* (a one-act sketch begun in 1839 and completed in 1842). Gogol is also known for his short stories, particularly *Diary of a Madman, The Nose and The Overcoat* and his novel *Dead Souls*.

Towards the end of his life, Gogol became tormented by religious guilt and as a result burnt the sequel he had written to his novel *Dead Souls*. Gogol died on March 4th 1852, his mind unbalanced, as a result of his refusal to eat.

SUMMARY OF THE PLOT

The corrupt officials of a remote Russian town, led by the Mayor, have fooled themselves into believing that Khlyestakov, who was staying at the local Hotel, is an important Government official (The Government Inspector of the title). Khlyestakov is in fact a penniless Government Clerk from St Petersburg, who was about to leave the hotel with his manservant, Ossip, without paying the bill. Khlyestakov has been persuaded to stay at the Mayor's house.

THE SCENE IN CONTEXT

In Scene One of this extract Khlyestakov has arrived with all of the town officials after visiting the hospital. In the events leading up to Scene Two of this extract, he has taken the opportunity to accept money from each of the town's officials who have been trying to get themselves into his good books. Khlyestakov is about to leave the town with all the money he has conned out of the local people, but takes the last opportunity to seduce both the Mayor's daughter, Maria, and his wife, Anna.

The Government Inspector

By

Nikolai Gogol – Russia

from an English version by Edward O. March and Jeremy Brooks

CAST LIST

MAYOR Anton Antonovich Skvoznnik Dmukhanovsky
KHLYESTAKOV a penniless clerk from Moscow, mistaken for the
    Government Inspector
MARIA the Mayor's daughter
ANNA the Mayor's wife and Maria's mother

(The Charity Commissioner, the Judge, the Schools Superintendent, the Postmaster, the Police Inspector, Dobchinsky and Bobchinsky (two landowners) are all present in Scene One and react to what Khlyestakov is saying and doing. For the purposes of staging this extract, these non-speaking roles can be omitted.)

Scene One

*A room in the **Mayor**'s house, shortly after lunch.*

***Khlyestakov** is drinking and being entertained by the **Mayor** and the other officials of the town. Enter **Anna** and **Maria**, resplendent.*

MAYOR Your honour, allow me to introduce… my wife, and my
    little daughter.

KHLYESTAKOV *bowing deeply* Madam, it is indeed a pleasure, if I may
    say so, to have the pleasure, as it were, of – er – meeting you!

ANNA *low curtsey* Our pleasure is much greater, Your Honour, in having so distinguished a guest!

KHLYESTAKOV *striking an attitude* No, 'pon my soul, Madam, on the contrary, my pleasure is far, far greater!

ANNA Oh, sir, now you're just being polite, I'm sure! Won't you please sit down?

KHLYESTAKOV Madam, simply to stand in such charming company is joy itself! However, if you insist, I'll sit. (*they sit on the sofa together*) Ah, what happiness it is for me to be sitting with you beside me!

ANNA I dare not think your words are anything but politeness, sir! Er … I imagine, sir, that life in the country must be very distasteful to you after life in Petersburg?

KHLYESTAKOV Oh, an unimaginable tediosity, Madam! When one is accustomed, comprenny-vous, to life in the best Society, suddenly to find oneself on the road, living in dirty inns amongst uncultured people…! If it weren't for my good fortune today… (*he looks up into* **Anna**'*s eyes*)… which, I assure you, makes up for everything…

ANNA It must all be so very unpleasant for you, sir.

KHLYESTAKOV At this moment, madam, everything is pleasantness itself!

ANNA Oh, how can you say such things! I'm not worthy of such compliments!

KHLYESTAKOV On the contrary, Madam, nobody could be more worthy!

ANNA But I live in the country…

KHLYESTAKOV And the country itself has its beauties – the woods, the hills, the sparkling streams… One can't, of course, compare it with Petersburg! Ça, c'est la vivre! You may be thinking that I'm only a clerk, but let me tell you the head of my department is very friendly with me! He'll slap me on the back, so, and say: "Come round for dinner, old chap" – just like that! I drop into the office for a few minutes, hand out a few instructions, and leave the old copy-clerk scratching away at his desk… They wanted to promote me, once, but I thought, "Ah, what's the use?" – and I turned it down. The office porter runs after me with his brush… "Allow me, Ivan Alexandrovich, allow me! I just want to shine your boots!" (*to the* **Mayor**) Why are you all still standing? Do sit down!

MAYOR *and* **others** We can stand…/That's all right, Your honour…/We know our rank…

KHLYESTAKOV Never mind your rank! Sit down! (*they all scurry to take a seat*) I won't have any standing on ceremony! I do everything I can, you know, to escape attention, but I'm afraid it's impossible. Wherever I turn up the word seems to get around at once. "There goes Ivan Alexandrovich Khlyestakov!" they say. Once I was actually mistaken for the Commander-in-Chief – yes! The soldiers all came dashing out of the guard room to present arms! And later their officer – who's actually a close friend of mine – said "D'you know, old chap, everyone was convinced you were the Commander-in-Chief!"

ANNA Well! Would you believe it!

KHLYESTAKOV It's quite true. Oh, and I know all the pretty actresses in town, of course. Well, you see, I've done quite a lot of writing for the stage… amusing little things… I go about a lot in the literary world… Pushkin's a close pal of mine. Whenever I see him I say, 'Well, Pushkin, old boy, how're things going with you?" And, do you know, he always says exactly the same thing: 'So-so, old chap," he says, "… only so-so." Ah, he's a great character, is Pushkin!

ANNA Are you really a writer, then? Oh, how wonderful it must be to be a writer! Do you ever write for the magazines?

KHLYESTAKOV Oh, yes, I publish in magazines, too. But then I do so many things: novels, plays… *Don Juan, Romeo and Juliet, The Marriage of Figaro* … I really can't remember all the titles. It was sheer chance that they came to be written anyway. Theatre managers were always pestering me – "Please, old chap, do write something for us, you know you can!" Eventually, just to get rid of them, I thought "All right, dammit, I will!" And I sat down, and do you know, I scribbled the whole lot in one evening! They were astonished, I can tell you. (*pause*) Yes, well. I've always had a very ready wit. All those pieces in *The Moscow Telegraph* under the name of Baron Brambeus – they're all mine.

ANNA No! Are you really Baron Brambeus?

KHLYESTAKOV Oh, yes. Why there's hardly a writer in the country whose work I haven't rewritten for him at one time or another – I get forty thousand a year doing that sort of thing.

ANNA I've just been reading a novel called *Youri Miloslavsky* –

KHLYESTAKOV Oh, yes, that's another of mine.

ANNA I knew it!

MARIA But Mamma, it says on the cover that it was written by Zagoskin!

ANNA You would have to argue, wouldn't you?

KHLYESTAKOV You're quite right, Madam, there is a book of that name by Zagoskin. But there is also one by me.

ANNA There! And I'm sure it was yours I read – it's so well written!

KHLYESTAKOV I must admit, I just live for literature! I keep the best house in Petersburg – everyone knows it, Khlyestakov House they call it. If you ever come to Petersburg, you must all come and see me! I give the grandest receptions you know!

ANNA I can imagine how magnificent they must be!

KHLYESTAKOV Oh, they're quite indescribable! In the centre of the table there'll be a huge water-melon costing seven hundred roubles. Then I have soup brought straight from Paris, by steamship, in special containers – you lift the lid, and that Parisienne aroma – ah, there's nothing like it in the world! I go to a dance or a reception everyday! ... ah, you should see my reception hall in the morning buzzing with counts and princes before I'm even awake... bzz, bzz, bzz... like a lot of bees, they are... Sometimes you'll even find the Prime Minister there, just hanging about, waiting for me... (*the **Mayor** and the **others** rise, awestruck*) My letters are all addressed to 'Your Excellency",

30

because I was once head of a whole Government department! Oh, yes! Very odd, that was. The director suddenly disappeared, no one knew where, and there were the usual squabbles over who should have the post. There were plenty of generals after the job, and some of them tried to do it, but it was no good, one after another they had to go, it was just too difficult. It looked simple enough at first sight, but when you got down to it, it needed real brains. So in the end they had to send for me. "Send for Ivan Alexandrovich," they said – and the messengers went out, all over Petersburg, messenger after messenger, all looking for me! Well, imagine it – thirty-five thousand messengers scurrying about, what about that, eh? "Ivan Alexandrovich," they cried when they found me, "come and take charge of the department!" I was staggered, I wanted to refuse, but then I thought, what if the Tsar heard about my refusal, he'd be offended! So I said to them, "All right," I said, "I'll do it," I said, "but I warn you, you'll have to watch out with me, I don't stand any nonsense from anyone…" And do you know, when I walked through that department you'd have thought there was an earthquake going on, they were all shaking and shivering so much with fear! (*the* **Mayor**, *etc., shiver.* **Khlyestakov** *gets more excited*) Oh, I won't be trifled with! I put the fear of God up them! I even had the Privy Council shaking in their shoes! Oh, yes! And why not, eh? That's the sort of man I am, not afraid of anybody. I tell them straight out, "Don't you try to stand in my way, my man!" And they don't! Because I can go anywhere – anywhere! I'm in and out of the Palace at all hours of the day and night – all hours! Why, tomorrow … tomorrow … they're going to make me … a… a Field Marshall! (*he slips and almost falls, but the* **Mayor** *and the* **others** *very respectfully support him*)

MAYOR *tries to speak but is trembling too much* Your … your … your …

KHLYESTAKOV *very sharp and abrupt* Well, what is it, what is it?

MAYOR Yo – Yo – Your –

KHLYESTAKOV *more sharply still* I can't understand a word, you're talking nonsense!

MAYOR Y-your lexcency – elxency – Exclensy … m-m-might w-w-want to l-l-lie down, have rest … your room's ready here, everything you need …

KHLYESTAKOV Lie down? Rest? Rubbish! Oh, all right, if you like, I suppose I might … that lunch was really very good, I'm much obleeged, much ob-leeged! (*he suddenly declaims*) Salted Cod! Salted Cod! SALTED COD! (*he nearly falls, but is helped out by the* **Mayor** *and the other* **officials**) (*All exit except* **Anna** *and* **Maria**)

ANNA What a fascinating man!

MARIA He's a darling!

ANNA He's so refined! You can see at once he's a man of fashion! Those lovely manners … beautiful gestures! I noticed he couldn't keep his eyes off me!

MARIA It was me he was looking at!

ANNA You? Don't be ridiculous, dear!

MARIA He was looking at me!

ANNA Why should he look at you? Can you tell me one reason on earth why he should look at you?

MARIA Well, he just did, that's all. When he started talking about his books he was looking straight at me, so there!

ANNA Well, maybe he did throw you a quick glance, but he was only being polite.

Enter the **Mayor** *on tiptoe.*

MAYOR Sssssh! Sssssh!

ANNA What's wrong?

MAYOR I wish I hadn't made him drunk. Suppose only half what he said was true? (*he thinks deeply*) And why shouldn't it be true? When a man's drunk the truth slips out, you can't prevent it. So he pops in and out of the Palace … dear God, I feel like a man on the gallows and no mistake.

ANNA I wasn't a bit frightened of him myself. To me he was just a man of real culture and breeding, that's all. I don't give a fig about his rank.

MAYOR Aaargh! Women! It's nothing but a game to you, is it? You with your silks and satins and feathers and flutters, if you drop a brick all you get is a good hiding from your husband – but your husband gets the sack! Don't you realise you were talking to him the way you talk to any Tom, Dick or Harry?

ANNA You worry too much, Antosha. We women know a thing or two, remember. (*Khlyestakov is heard coughing from the next room*)

MAYOR Ssssh! (*he walks on tiptoe to listen at* **Khlyestakov's** *door. The end of the scene is played in whispers*) Not a sound, now d'you hear! Run along now, you've chattered quite enough.

ANNA Come on then, Mashenka. There's one fascinating thing I noticed about our guest … I'll tell you as soon as we're alone. (*she sweeps out,* **Maria** *following*)

MAYOR Talk, talk, talk – women'll talk your ears right off!

Black out.

End of Scene One

Scene Two

A room in the **Mayor**'s *house. The next day.*

Khlyestakov *is calling off stage at one door, enter* **Maria** *from the inner door.*

KHLYESTAKOV *calling off* Ossip! The horses!

MARIA *girlishly startled* Oh!

KHLYESTAKOV Why so frightened, may I ask?

MARIA I wasn't frightened, really …

KHLYESTAKOV Allow me to say, dear lady, I would be delighted to think you might have thought I would think that you … hrchm … (*striking an attitude*) May I ask where you were going?

MARIA Why, I wasn't going anywhere, really.

KHLYESTAKOV And why were you not going anywhere, really, dear lady?

MARIA I thought perhaps Mamma was in here.

KHLYESTAKOV Of course. But your real reason …?

MARIA *hedging* I'm being a nuisance. I'm sure you've got some awfully important business to attend to.

KHLYESTAKOV *posturing again* What business could ever be as important to me, dear lady, as looking into your incomparable eyes? You couldn't possibly be a nuisance, your presence could only be a pleasure!

MARIA The way you talk! Just like real society!

KHLYESTAKOV To such a gorgeous creature as yourself, how else should I talk? May I have the extreme happiness of offering you a chair? Only you should not have a simple chair, but a throne!

MARIA I don't know. I think I ought to be going. (*but she sits down*)

KHLYESTAKOV What a beautiful scarf you're wearing!

MARIA Oh! Go on, you're making fun of me! Just because I'm a provincial …!

KHLYESTAKOV How I would love to be that scarf, nestling so closely round you lily-white neck.

MARIA What are you talking about? Wanting to be a scarf …! What strange weather we're having today.

KHLYESTAKOV Your lips, dear lady, are stranger and more inscrutably fascinating than any weather!

MARIA Won't you write some verses for my album – I'm sure you know lots of verses, don't you?

KHLYESTAKOV For you – I could do anything. Ask, and it will be done! What sort of verses would you like?

MARIA Something … well, you know, something good. Something new.

KHLYESTAKOV Oh, verses, verses … I know so many of them!

MARIA Won't you recite some, then?

KHLYESTAKOV But why? I can write them down without all that.

MARIA I'm fond of listening to poems …

KHLYESTAKOV Well, I know dozens of them, dozens.

MARIA Well, go on!

KHLYESTAKOV Well, if you insist, here's one of mine I might put in your album – 'Shall I compare thee to a summer's day? Thou art more lovely and more temperate; Rough winds do shake de dum de dum de dum' And so on and so forth – that's one of my sonnets. I've done lots more, lots, I just can't remember the words this instant. Oh, but what do poems matter, I'd much rather speak of the love I feel when I gaze into your beautiful eyes … (*he draws his chair closer to her*)

MARIA Love! Oh, I don't know anything about that (*she edges her chair away*)

KHLYESTAKOV *moving up again* Why do you move away? It's much nicer being close together!

MARIA *moving away* I think it's nicer (*she shifts*) further (*she shifts*) away.

KHLYESTAKOV *closer* But there's no need to move away. You only imagine we're close. You could just as well imagine we're far apart. Ah, but how happy I would be, dear lady, if I could enfold you in my arms …

MARIA *looking suddenly out of the window* Oh, look! What sort of bird was that? Was it a magpie?

KHLYESTAKOV *kissing her shoulder* Here's a magpie!

MARIA *jumping up indignantly* No, really, that's too much!

KHLYESTAKOV *holding her back* Forgive me, Ma'am, please forgive me! It was only my great love made me do it, only my love …

MARIA You think just because I'm a country girl you can … (*she tries to get away*)

KHLYESTAKOV *still holding her* No! it was love, I swear to you, I meant no harm, it was only my unconquerable love! Oh, forgive me, forgive me, Maria Antonovna, I'll go down on my knees to you if you'll forgive me! (*he falls on his knees*) Look, look, I'm on my knees before you!

Enter **Anna Andreyevna**.

ANNA Well! This is a surprise! (*to Maria*) What does all this mean, then? That's a fine way to behave, I'm sure!

MARIA Really, Mamma. It wasn't …

ANNA Leave the room this instant! Go on, run along! And don't you dare show your face in here again! (*Maria goes off in tears*) I'm sorry, Your Honour, but really – well, it was a surprise!

KHLYESTAKOV *aside* She's quite fetching herself – hm, hm, not bad at all … (*he shuffles towards her on his knees*) Oh, Madame, Madame, can't you see that I'm dying of love!

ANNA Oh, do get up, sir, the floor's filthy!

KHLYESTAKOV No, no, on my knees … I must stay on my knees … 'til I hear my fate … Is it to be life … or death?

ANNA I don't know what you're carrying on about, really I don't. are you making a declaration about my daughter?

KHLYESTAKOV No, no, it's you I'm in love with, you! My whole life is at stake, for if you can't return my undying love then I'm not worthy of life at all! My heart is on fire as I beg for your hand …!

ANNA But sir, I must point out that I am – er – in a manner of speaking – er – married.

KHLYESTAKOV Married! What is a marriage! True love knows nothing of these formalities! As the poet said – 'Tis but itself the law condemns!'

ANNA They do say 'True love can leap the fastest torrent'.

KHLYESTAKOV Of course it can, beloved lady! We'll fly together, hand in hand, to the banks of some gurgling brook ... Your hand, I beg you, your hand!

*Enter **Maria**, running.*

MARIA Mamma, Pappa says you're to ... (*she cries out as she sees Khylestakov on his knees*) Well, what a surprise!

ANNA What are you doing here, you little fidget, dashing in like a scalded cat, I thought I told you to keep out? What's a surprise, eh? I don't know what nonsense you've got in your head now, you're just like a child, no one would guess you were eighteen years old!

MARIA *in tears* But Mamma, I didn't know ...

ANNA You don't know nothing, that's your trouble, always in a whirl, just like those Lyapkin-Tyapkin girls, can't you find a better model than them? You could take your mother as an example, for instance, couldn't you?

KHLYESTAKOV *taking **Maria**'s hand* Anna Andreyevna, I beg you not to oppose our happiness! Give your blessing to our love!

ANNA *astonished* What? You mean – it's her?

*Heavy winking from **Khlyestakov**.*

KHLYESTAKOV Tell me quickly – is it life – or death?

ANNA *turning on **Maria*** There, you see, you stupid girl? Just for the sake of a silly little baggage like you, His Excellency has to go down on his knees to me! And then of course you have to burst in like a lunatic ... It would serve you right if I said no, just to teach you a lesson. You don't deserve such luck!

MARIA I won't do it again, Mamma, I promise.

*Enter **Mayor**, breathless.*

MAYOR Your Excellency, mercy! Have mercy on me!

KHLYESTAKOV Now what's the matter?

MAYOR Those shopkeepers have been making complaints about me, I know they have, and it's all lies, not half of it's true, they're cheats and liars, the lot of them, they're always giving short measure and that. And that Sergeant's widow said I had her flogged; it's a rotten lie, she flogged herself!

KHLYESTAKOV Oh to hell with the Sergeant's widow, I've got other things to think about!

MARIA Pappa, His Excellency has asked …

MAYOR Don't you believe a word of it, Your Honour! They're just a pack of rotten liars!

MARIA Pappa, I think His Excellency wants to ask …

ANNA Be quiet, girl! Do you know the honour Ivan Alexandrovich is doing us, my dear? He's asked for our daughter's hand in marriage!

MAYOR What?! You're out of your mind, woman! Don't be angry with her, Your Excellency, she's a bit weak in the head. Her mother was just the same.

KHLYESTAKOV But I really am asking your consent to my marrying your daughter. I love her!

MAYOR I don't believe it.

KHLYESTAKOV You must give us your consent! I'm desperate. I could do something awful if you refuse … and then my blood would be on your hands!

MAYOR No, no, please, I'm innocent, I haven't done a thing; I swear it…. Yes, anything Your Excellency pleases. Oh, God! What am I saying? My head's going round!

ANNA For pity's sake, give them your blessing, then! (**Khlyestakov** *approaches the* **Mayor**, *leading* **Maria** *by the hand*)

MAYOR May God bless you both, I suppose, but none of it's my fault, I'm entirely innocent, you know. (**Khlyestakov** *kisses* **Maria**. *The* **Mayor** *is still puzzled*) Hey, look, they're kissing each other!

(*the **Mayor** rubs his eyes and stares*) It's true! Is it true? It's true they're engaged! (*the **Mayor** dances with joy*) What about that, Anton! Three cheers for the Mayor! What a stroke of genius!

VOICE *offstage* The horses are ready, sir.

KHLYESTAKOV Ah … right. Coming now.

MAYOR What's that? Horses? Are you leaving?

KHLYESTAKOV That's right.

MAYOR But didn't I understand …? Your Excellency was pleased to hint – er – possible marriage?

KHLYESTAKOV Oh, I shan't be away a minute, well, that is, no more than a day… to see my uncle, you know, very rich uncle, have to get his blessing too, of course. I'll be back tomorrow.

MAYOR We wouldn't presume to keep you, of course. We can only await the happiness of your return.

KHLYESTAKOV That's right. Good. Well, I'll be back in no time. Goodbye, my darling … oh, I can't find words to express all I feel! Goodbye, beloved, my love, my darling, goodbye … (*he kisses **Maria**'s hand*)

MAYOR Is there nothing you need for the road, Your Excellency? You were a little short of ready money …

KHLYESTAKOV No, no, what on earth made you think … (*pause*) Yes, well, perhaps I am – a bit short.

MAYOR How much do you need?

KHLYESTAKOV Let's see now, you lent me two hundred- no of course, it was four, I mustn't take advantage of your mistake, must I? So if you could just let me have the same again, that would make a round eight hundred, wouldn't it?

MAYOR Certainly, certainly! (*he produces notes*) There, all in nice crisp new notes!

KHLYESTAKOV Really! (*he takes the notes and examines them*) Very nice too. They say new banknotes bring you luck don't they?

MAYOR Indeed they do.

KHLYESTAKOV Well, goodbye then, Anton Antonovich. Thanks for all your hospitality. I can say quite sincerely that I've never been so well received – anywhere, ever before, never! Goodbye, Anna Andreyevna! And farewell, my darling Maria Antonova! My heart's desire! Goodbye! (*Khlyestakov and the Mayor go out together*)

KHLYESTAKOV *off stage* Goodbye, all!

MAYOR *off stage* When can we expect Your Excellency back?

KHLYESTAKOV *off stage* Tomorrow or the next day.

DRIVER *off stage* Whoa-up!

KHLYESTAKOV *off stage* Goodbye, Anton Antonovich. Goodbye, all!

ANNA *and* **Maria** *at the window* Goodbye, Ivan Alexandrovich!

KHLYESTAKOV *off stage* Goodbye, Mamma! Goodbye my angel! Goodbye, Pappa!

DRIVER *off stage* Giddyap, giddyap! (*the sound of the horses and carriage fade into the distance. **Anna** and **Maria** embrace and shed a tear for the man they love. The **Mayor** returns and looks at them both*)

MAYOR Well, who have thought it, eh, Anna? Our daughter marrying an important person like that?

Black out.

Staging the extract

SET DESIGN

The setting for the two scenes in the extract is the drawing room of the Mayor's house. The staging can be elaborate with real attention to detail in terms of the period and set dressing or kept to a minimum. In Adrian Mitchell's version of the play, written for the National Theatre in 1985, the setting is described as, "a warm, plush room, somewhat over decorated with oil paintings, screens, busts etc. The high bourgeois style of the 1830s." In other versions it is translated simply as *A room in the Mayor's House*. It is possible to stage the scenes therefore in a simple way with the following basic requirements:

- a large entrance door that leads to the outside of the house
- a door that leads to the interior of the house
- an optional second door that leads to the guest room
- a window looking outside into the street
- at least two chairs or a large sofa.

Because *The Government Inspector* was written for the early 19th Century Russian Theatre, it was originally staged on a Proscenium Arch stage probably with large entrance doors upstage centre and entrances down stage left and right. In a studio setting you can dispense with complicated scenery altogether by staging the extract in-the-round with the audience on all four sides of the action. The gangways between the four blocks of audience become the entrances and exits onto the acting area.

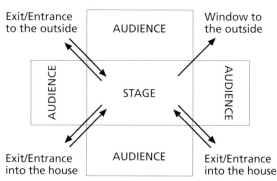

The stage can be more circular in shape than in the diagram and the audience can be seated in a circle with gangways through the seats for entrances and exits.

You will need to consider:

- How can you ensure that all the audience will be able to see all of the action?
- How might you use floor covering to define the acting space?
- What props will you need and how can they help to give the right feel to the setting?

COSTUMES

A flamboyant Khlyestakov seeking to seduce Maria.

Gogol provides the following costume notes for three of the characters in this extract:

THE MAYOR: He is normally dressed in the frock-coat of his official uniform, of which the most striking features are the buttons and button-holes. In addition to this he wears spurred and highly polished jack-boots.

KHLYESTAKOV: He dresses very fashionably.

ANNA: She has four complete changes of costume during the play.

With all of the costumes you will need to think about the time period within which you choose to set the play. As the characters are meant to be larger than life you will need to think carefully about the style, shape and colour of the costumes. Although Khlyestakov's clothes may be fashionable, they will be inexpensive, well worn and/or second-hand.

Of the four costume changes mentioned above for Anna, two of them happen in this extract. Maria will also certainly require two costumes so as not to be out done by her mother. You will need to find two different dresses for each of the characters that are patterned, brightly coloured and that will be noticed. The stage direction for Scene One of the extract describes them as being "resplendent" which suggests that they have gone to a lot of trouble over their appearance. Maria's second costume requires a scarf because Khlystetakov "would love to be that scarf, nestling so closely round your lily-white neck." The clues to the kind of clothes that Anna and Maria wear are in a section of dialogue in a scene prior to the extract. Anna insists that Maria wears her "pale blue with the little flounces" and says that she will wear her "primrose". They go off arguing, with Maria wanting to wear her "marigold".

Exploring the extract

HISTORICAL AND CULTURAL CONTEXT

The Russia of Gogol's time was a country ruled by the Tsar. There was a great divide between the rich and poor with a whole section of society that was born into Serfdom. Serfdom was a form of lawful slavery whereby a servant was attached to a particular property or land and worked for the owner of that land. If the owner sold the land, the Serf had to be sold as part of the deal and was therefore guaranteed continued employment.

The influence of Western Europe on early 19th century Russian Theatre is apparent from Gogol's own writings:

'The situation of the Russian actor is pitiful. All about him a young nation pulsates and seethes and they give him characters he has never set eyes upon. What can he do with these strange heroes, who are neither Frenchmen nor Germans but bizarre people totally devoid of definite passions and distinct features? Where can he display his art? On what can he develop his talent? For heaven's sake give us Russian characters, give us ourselves – our scoundrels, our eccentrics ..."

This is exactly what Gogol gives his actors and his audience in *The Government Inspector*. Rather than using the plays of France and Germany as models, Gogol sets about writing a truly Russian play peopled with characters from his own country.

◆1a **Discussion**

To what extent do you think plays, novels, films and/or television plays you have seen are influenced by other cultures?

cont...

> To paraphrase Gogol, it could be said that, "all about you pulsates and seethes a vibrant multi-cultural Britain but all you are given is a diet of American culture."
>
> How can you identify what it is like to be British today in things that you read, watch or listen to?

GENRE AND SUBJECT MATTER

The Government Inspector is a difficult play to categorise: there is no doubt that the play is a comedy, but Gogol condemned the first production for turning it into a broad farce. The central theme of mistaken identity is a common one that can be found in Roman Comedy and in the plays of Shakespeare for example. It is Gogol's treatment of the theme that makes it different because he uses it to create a satire on corruption in local government. Gogol was attempting to create a new kind of social realism by putting the kinds of people he had observed in local government on the stage.

◆1b Discussion

What do the words realism and satire mean?

DRAMA TECHNIQUES

◆1c Dialogue chairs exercise

16 One of the moments of comic business in Scene Two of this extract is when Khlyestakov and Maria are both sat on chairs and as he moves his chair closer to hers she moves hers away from him.

In pairs

Organisation: Two actors start off on chairs with a gap between them, each holding their chair underneath so that they can stand and walk with the chair beneath them and then sit down again.

Situation: Actor A has to say things about how much they like Actor B and Actor B has to respond by not really believing what they are saying. Each time Actor A speaks he/she moves her chair right next to Actor B and when Actor B responds, he/she moves away again. Actor B should try out moving different distances and stopping and starting between words in their response.

Opening Line: **ACTOR A** You know your hands are like an artist's hands, so delicate and fine.

Once you have explored the comic potential of this business, you can apply the techniques to the dialogue between Khlyestakov and Maria that starts:

KHLYESTAKOV I'd much rather speak of the love I feel when I gaze into your beautiful eyes... and finishes:

MARIA No, really, that's too much.

◆1d The unexpected exercise

There are two moments in Scene Two when the characters encounter situations that they did not expect to walk in on. Anna walks in to find Khlyestakov on his knees before her daughter, Maria, and the reverse happens when Maria runs in to find Khlyestakov on his knees before her mother and holding her hand.

In groups

1. *Organisation:* The group is given a situation and has to create a tableau or **freeze-frame** to illustrate it. One or more people, in the role of observers, leave the room once they have seen the freeze-frame. The group left in the room then has to do something unexpected with the freeze-frame that they have created.

   Situation: The group could start, for example, with a hold-up in the bank and transform it into a ballroom dancing lesson.

   The idea of the exercise is for the observers to come back into the room and see the "freeze-frame" that they left and as soon as they enter the room, the "freeze-frame" is turned into the unexpected. The group watches the observer's reaction to the change and slowly put the freeze-frame back to its original state. In a similar way this is the way that Anna and Maria have to react in Scene Two.

Exploring characters

THE MAYOR

These are Gogol's notes on the Mayor's character:

> His hair has turned grey in the government service but in his way he is far from being a fool. He takes bribes but still manages to keep a certain measure of dignity. He is quite a serious person, something of a moralist, in fact. What he says is never too much, never too little; when he does speak it is never too loud, never too soft, and yet his every word is heavy with meaning. His features are as coarse and cruel as those of any successful person who has begun at the bottom in a difficult service. He veers rapidly from fear to joy, from subservience to arrogance, as befits a man with scarcely developed spiritual feelings. His hair is short and grizzled.

◆1e Emotion and Behaviour Scales

- Gogol suggests that the Mayor's emotions and behaviour change very quickly.

  Using the following "Emotion scale", go through each of the Mayor's lines and decide what state he is in for each line. Mark a line E1 if you think he is fearful , progressing through to E5 if you think he is joyful.

FEAR ←				→ JOY
E1	E2	E3	E4	E5

- Using the following "Behaviour scale", go through each of the Mayor's lines and decide how he is behaving for each line. Mark a line B1 if you think he is being subservient, progressing through to B5 if you think he is being arrogant.

SUBSERVIENT				ARROGANT
B1	B2	B3	B4	B5

- What does this exercise tell you about the Mayor's character?
- How is his behaviour towards his Wife and Daughter different to the way he behaves towards Khlyestakov?

ANNA

These are Gogol's notes on Anna's character:

Anna Andreyevna is a provincial coquette, not exactly old yet, whose education has been about equally divided between romantic novels and anthology verse. Her main concerns are the pantry and the servants. She is extremely inquisitive and her vanity is displayed at every turn. She now and then gets the upper hand of her husband simply because he is not ready for an answer. She uses this power only for trivial things, however, lecturing him and sneering at him turn and turn about.

◆1f Discussion

- What is a coquette? Find examples in the extract, which show Anna behaving in this way.
- Do you admire the way Anna behaves? What does she hope to achieve from the way she behaves with Khlyestakov?
- What is it about Khlyestakov that she finds attractive? What did she find attractive in her husband? Are the qualities the same or different?

If you are playing the part of Anna, it is very easy to play her as a caricature by using exaggerated movements and an outrageous voice. How will you avoid this and create a real person that an audience can believe in?

KHLYESTAKOV

These are Gogol's notes on Khlyestakov's character:

> A young man of twenty-three – slender, not to say thin. He tends to be silly, to the extent even, as the saying goes, of being 'not quite all there' – the sort of person his fellow workers in the same office consider a dead loss. He speaks and acts without a thought for anything or anybody. He is quite incapable of giving his undivided attention to any single idea. His speech is convulsive, the words jerk out in a totally unexpected fashion. The more simple and ingenuous the actor can appear in this part the better he will be.

The role of Khlyestakov demands a lot of energy and stamina and an actor with real presence on stage. Khlyestakov does not deliberately pretend to be a Government Inspector but he is quite happy to go along with pretending that he is one once he realises that the Townspeople have mistaken him for one. During Scene One of the extract he just gets carried away with his own invention and in Scene Two he successfully manages to seduce Maria so that he just tries the same trick with Anna.

◆1g You'll never believe who I met...

In pairs or as a group

11

Look at Khlyestakov's speech that begins, "Oh, they're quite indescribable..." and notice the exaggerated way in which he goes on to describe his life in St Petersburg.

1. *Organisation:* One person is in the role of Khlyestakov and the partner or the rest of the group is listening to the story.

   Situation: Khlyestakov is telling one of his exaggerated accounts. His listener must believe and accept what the person playing Khlyestakov is saying and reply with a positive statement like, "Oh, really, what were they like?" The improvisation should then build from here so that Khlyestakov can get away with saying almost anything he likes to make himself sound magnificent and important.

Opening Line: **KHLYESTAKOV** When I was staying in St Petersburg (or the name of any famous town or city) I met _____ (the name of a famous person).

Go back to the original speech and try and capture the same sense of spontaneity you created in the improvisation when you act out the dialogue.

◆1h Discussion

- Khlyestakov could be described as nothing more than a liar and a thief, but why is he so difficult to dislike?
- Would you fall for someone like Khlyestakov and be taken in by him?
- How do you know whether someone is being honest and truthful to you or not?
- What would you say to someone like Khlyestakov once you found out that they were not who you thought they were?

MARIA

Gogol does not provide any character notes for Maria, but in many ways she is a younger version of her mother. Her mother has taught her everything she knows and she has led a sheltered existence.

◆1i Comparing Characters

1. Draw two columns on a sheet of paper and put Anna's name at the top of the left hand column and Maria's name at the top of the right hand column. Under Anna's name, list the adjectives, facts and details that best describe her character.

2. In the Maria column, next to each of the Anna adjectives, put "yes" if you think the adjective also describes Maria, "no" if it does not and "yes/no" if it partially does.

cont...

Review your list and add any additional adjectives, facts or details to Maria's column that are unique to her. Discuss the similarities and differences between Maria and her Mother. How would you show this in performance if you were acting the role of Maria? As an acting exercise, the actor playing Maria, should have a go at playing the part of Anna and then go back to playing her own lines to see what effect this has.

COMPARING TEXTS

◆1j Theme for comparison: Parent-child relationships

The common subject matter that runs through the four plays in this collection is about the role and influence that parents have on their children. In *The Government Inspector,* Maria is a young adult still living at home with her mother and father. Maria is more like a companion and friend to her mother than a daughter but this does not prevent either Anna treating Maria like a child or Maria behaving like one. The normal order of parental relationships is thrown into chaos when both Mother and Daughter have the same love interest in Khlyestakov.

1. How does Anna's attitude to her daughter getting married compare with that of Badua's attitude in *Anowa*? How is the subject dealt with differently?

2. Does the Mayor have anything in common with the father (Eric) in *Summer of the Aliens* and the father (Osam) in *Anowa*? Are there any noticeable differences between these three characters in their attitudes to their daughters/son?

◆1k Writing

H Imagine that you are Khlyestakov and that you have arrived back in St Petersburg with a story to tell.

Write a letter to a friend telling them all about the events that happened to you in the small town and about the people that you met there.

Write an article for the **Moscow Telegraph** about the goings on in a small Russian town that is miles away from the capital. The headline might read: CORRUPTION IN THE COUNTRY.

Summer of the Aliens

Louis Nowra

LOUIS NOWRA

Louis Nowra was born in Melbourne, Australia on 12th December 1949. At the age of 14, Louis suffered a severe accident which caused him to lose most of the sight in his left eye and his ability to speak properly.

At the age of 17, Nowra studied English at La Trobe University in Melbourne but never finished the course. After giving up his University course, Nowra had several jobs , became involved in Street Theatre and began writing scripts. One of these Street Theatre scripts (*Kiss the One-Eyed Priest*) was accepted by the La Mama Theatre in Melbourne and produced there in 1973. A steady output of plays for the stage, radio and film continued from this point on making Louis Nowra one of Australia's most important writers. In 1996, Nowra was awarded an Honorary Doctorate degree from Griffith University for his "distinguished contribution to literature." Some of Nowra's other plays include, *The Golden Age* (1985) *Radiance* (1993 and filmed in 1997, directed by Rachel Perkins) and the sequel to *Summer of the Aliens, Cosi* (1992 and filmed in 1995, directed by Mark Joffe).

Summer of the Aliens was first performed by the Melbourne Theatre Company at the Russell Street Theatre, Melbourne on 17th March 1992.

SUMMARY OF THE PLOT

Summer of the Aliens is about the journey of the 14 year old Lewis from adolescence into manhood. The older Lewis in the role of a Narrator tells the story of the events in 1962 when he was growing up in a Melbourne housing estate. The young Lewis only thinks about flying saucers and the sounds of aliens he hears in the telegraph wires. His friend Brian on the other hand can only think about losing his virginity, whilst his tomboy friend, Dulcie, tries every which way she can to seduce him. Meanwhile the world is faced with the Cuban Missile crisis and is almost on the verge of a nuclear war. The play is full of odd characters like Mr Pisano the postman who complains that he cannot read the house numbers in the street so sets about painting huge numbers on people's doors, and Beatrice a Dutch girl who can only use swear words when she speaks English. To Lewis all this strange behaviour can only mean one thing: the Aliens are among them.

THE SCENE IN CONTEXT

One of the key events in Lewis' life in this year is the sudden return of his father, Eric, after a three-year absence. Eric left his wife, Norma, to bring up their son, Lewis, and their daughter, Bev, by herself as well as looking after her own mother who has moved in with Sam her pet budgerigar. These scenes deal with the story of Eric's return as if he had never been away.

Summer of the Aliens

By

Louis Nowra – Australia

CAST LIST

NARRATOR – the older Lewis
NORMA – Lewis' mother
ERIC – Lewis' father
LEWIS – 14 years old

Setting

A Housing Commission Estate in the paddocks of northern Melbourne in 1962 at the time of the Cuban missile crisis.

Scene One

The backyard. **Lewis** *practising his bowling.*

NARRATOR In the long, hot Australian summer days there are signs of movement. And there I am, practising my bowling. The earth is cracked, the grass is dead and the stumps is one of the washing line posts in the backyard. There are two posts, a couple of metres high, with clothes lines tied to both crossbars, so that the lines look like crucifixes. The ball, its leaving the hand, its drift and spin through the hot hair, its fall and turn once it hits the ground is mesmerising. I bowl through the long afternoons thinking I am a famous cricketer. I'm thinking of a cat dying, Dulcie and her knife against my throat, she showing her breasts to Brian, Mrs Irvin and her piece of St Thomas's bone …

A distant song is heard sung by a man.

ERIC Many a tear has to fall
　　　But it's all in the game
　　　All in the wonderful game of love.

*A man appears. It is **Eric**, **Lewis'** father.*

LEWIS Dad!

ERIC Hi, kid! You had words with him
　　　And your future's looking dim
　　　But these things your heart
　　　Will fly above.

He kisses him and guides him into the house. They are happy. He keeps on singing.

　　　Once in a while he won't call
　　　But it's all in the game.

NARRATOR My mother always said that when he first dated her he would come singing *It's all in the Game* and leave at night singing *Carrickfergus*.

ERIC Soon he'll be there
　　　With a small bouquet
　　　And he'll kiss your lips
　　　And caress your fingertips
　　　And your heart will fly away.

NARRATOR He was back after three years. He hadn't changed that much. We children were glad to have him home, unlike my grandmother and, of course, my mother. (*pause*) I heard them in her bedroom that night. The door was open.

Scene Two

The bedroom. Night.

NORMA I didn't hear a word from you. You sent no money.

ERIC Yes, I did.

NORMA Once. What were you doing?

ERIC Digging tunnels.

NORMA Tunnels?

ERIC The Snowy Mountains scheme.

NORMA You know nothing about tunnels.

ERIC I do now.

NORMA What did you do with the money you earned?

ERIC Caught the gambling bug.

NORMA Was there another woman?

ERIC There's always been only you.

NORMA Come off it.

ERIC Only you.

NORMA Why did you leave then?

ERIC Felt suffocated, I guess.

NORMA Suffocated? You say, one day, that you're going out to get a screw for the shower and don't come back. I was worried frantic. The police came and everything. They were quite certain. "He's run off," they said, "probably didn't like being a husband". Nice coming from the police, isn't it?

ERIC They were wrong.

NORMA You ran away because of the children and me.

ERIC I've come back.

NORMA Hip hooray, let's strike up the band! (*pause*) You must hate me to do what you did.

ERIC There's so many of you. You, the kids, now your mother's here.

NORMA Because she pays board. (*a beat*) You left because you hate me, you hate your children.

ERIC I don't hate anyone. I just got itchy feet.

NORMA Have you no sense of responsibility? (*a beat*)

ERIC Guess not. (*pause*)

NORMA What are you going to do?

ERIC Don't know. Might level the backyard –

NORMA Level the backyard?

ERIC You've always been after me to do it.

NORMA You can't stay here, I don't want you any more. (*a beat*)

ERIC The kids liked me being back.

NORMA Of course, they've forgotten what you're really like. They don't know how shiftless and lazy you are!

ERIC I'm not that. I've changed my ways.

NORMA Shhhh…

She's looking at the doorway. He turns to see what she's staring at. It is **Lewis** *looking at them.*

NORMA What are you doing up at this hour, love?

LEWIS Couldn't sleep.

NORMA How long have you been standing there?

LEWIS Not long.

ERIC Why can't you sleep?

LEWIS Asthma.

NORMA How's your spray?

LEWIS You staying, dad?

ERIC Depends on your mother. I mean, your mum's been a wiz looking after you while I've been working. (*she gives a small snort of derision*) An absolute Wiz. The Wiz of Oz.

Scene Three

Night. **Eric** *is sitting under the house with a torch humming to himself* It's all in the Game. **Lewis** *crawls under also carrying a torch.*

LEWIS Dad … dad …

ERIC Over here. And keep your voice down.

LEWIS Why are we under the house?

ERIC Shhhh … Listen. Your mother's footsteps. Pretty heavy for a small woman. You can hear your grannie snoring. Women hate being underground. It scares them. That's why men love being underground. Be away from women. You should have seen the tunnels we dug in the Snowy Mountains. Right through granite like a knife through butter. Day after day we blew up the rock with dynamite, inching our way down for the good of Australia. It got hotter as we got deeper. We dug past fossils from dinosaur days. It was hard to breathe it was so deep. A lot of strange things happen in tunnels.

LEWIS What sort of thing?

ERIC Can't go into details right now. (*a beat*) When you're older. We could dig a tunnel – just the two of us – under the house and come out under the Irvin's floorboards. Boy, would they be surprised. That girl you like, Dulcie or whatever, you could come up through her bedroom floor. Her eyes would be as big as saucers. (*he starts to crawl under the house with the torch, exploring the space*) A lot of space … We could dig a tunnel through the floorboards into Castro's bedroom, probably while he's knocking off some Russian sheila.

LEWIS What exactly are we doing, dad?

ERIC We're being quiet, that's what we're doing. (*footsteps above*) I can always tell your mother's footsteps. Doesn't realise what we've got in store for her. Women always expect the worst from a man.

A pause as they listen to **Norma** *singing a snatch of a song.*

NORMA   Step we gaily on we go
        heel and heel
        and toe for toe
        arm and arm
        and row and row
        all for Marie's wedding.

ERIC   *a pause as they listen to the footsteps* Bit of a bounce in her 59
footsteps. Probably thinking of me. Hey, it's lucky we're white,
isn't it? How do blacks see one another in the dark? Like those
West Indian cricketers eh? I saw them in the tied Test.

LEWIS   I thought you were in the Snowy Mountains?

ERIC   I was up in Brisbane for a while. Had to see a man about a
tunnel. The West Indians were like gods. (*stopping, looking around*)
A lot of work ahead of us. Our little Snowy Scheme right under
your mother's feet. Twinkle, twinkle little star, sixteen days and
there you are. Always remember that rhyme, Lewis. It's how long
it took Bert Hinkler to fly to Australia from London. My father
taught it to me. You know what happened in the Second World
War? (**Lewis** *shakes his head*) Those fellers wanted to escape from
the Nazis, so they built a wooden horse, an exercise horse, to dig
a tunnel. The problem was: how to get rid of the soil so that the
krauts didn't know what was happening. So they put the soil up
their trousers and secretly sprinkled it on the parade ground.
That's us, Lewis. We're the POWS and your mum's the kraut. In
sixteen days we're going to give her the bestest birthday present.

Scene Four

The front yard of a neighbour's house. Night. **Eric** *has a wheelbarrow.
He enters, looking for the perfect spot to dig, then realising that* **Lewis** *is
straggling reluctantly, signals for him to hurry up. Carting a spade,* **Lewis**
enters.

ERIC   *gazing at stars* Twinkle, twinkle little star
                Sixteen days and there you are.

LEWIS   People will see us.

ERIC   They're watching TV or are asleep.

LEWIS But they'll notice what we've done.

ERIC It's not as if we're going to excavate the whole bloody front yard. We're nicking a bit from here, from the Johnson's, the Boyles.

LEWIS But we'll leave a hole.

ERIC Not a big one. They'll come out in the morning and think it was some animal.

LEWIS What happens if we're caught?

ERIC We'll say we're digging trenches as a last ditch stand against the Commies.

Hey, how do you greet an American?

LEWIS Don't know.

ERIC *shaking* **Lewis**' *hand* How ya doin', Yankee. How do you greet a Commie? (**Lewis** *holds out his hand to be shaken*) Like this! (**Eric** *grabs his son by the arm and swings him over his shoulder, causing* **Lewis** *to land on his back with a thud.*

Lewis *is winded.* **Eric** *puts his foot on* **Lewis**' *chest.*)

Give up, Commie?

LEWIS *winded* Yes.

ERIC Like Commies, weak as piss. And what's the first lesson?

LEWIS Don't know, dad.

ERIC Never shake hands with a Communist unless you mean to do him harm. (*holding out hand*) Come on, get up, we haven't much time. (**Lewis** *reaches for his hand suspiciously and his father lifts him up in one strong, violent pull*) Sixteen days it is then. Fifteen now. Fifteen nights. We nick the Merri Creek soil from all the front yards that have it then store it under our house. Night of your mum's birthday we level the backyard until it's as smooth as a baby's bum and flat as a billiard table. Don't you want to do that for your mum? (**Lewis** *nods*) Besides, we can build a cricket pitch on it. We'll be killing two birds with one stone. (*a beat*) Dig, you dig?

NARRATOR *as* **Lewis** *digs* So, over the following night we stole soil from our neighbours' front yards. My father telling me stories of the Snowy Mountains, tunnelling from Victoria into New South Wales and of a dago trying to kill him with a dinosaur bone.

ERIC Hang on. Let's rest a moment. You don't want to work like a wog, do you? They even worked through smokos. Had to take to them with a jack hammer. They could tell I wasn't scared of them when one of them tried to brain me with a dinosaur bone. (*looking around at the lawn*) Pisano is a bit of a nutter, isn't he? I saw him mowing his lawn this morning but he's sort of just done bits of it. Holy Toledo! You know what he's done. He's mown a giant 45 into his lawn.

LEWIS It's the number of his house. It's to teach the rest of the neighbourhood a lesson, he said.

ERIC He's definitely not the full quid. This is good though, eh?

LEWIS What?

ERIC Us two. Father and son. Unnatural to have women around all the time. That thing between your legs, Lewis. Women go, 'Oh, no, no!' but they always want it. Get them up the duff and it's our fault. You never hear the end of it. (**Lewis** *looks around, hearing something*) What is it?

LEWIS The telephone wires. It's like singing, isn't it? (**Eric** *listens, he cannot understand his son's pleasure*)

ERIC You're hearing things. You're at a difficult age. Your mum said Uncle Richard had a word to you.

LEWIS He said I should marry a girl from Asia.

ERIC Christ, we fought the slant eyes during the war and now he wants you to marry them. Forget it: he's a bit of a poof anyway. The important things are practical things. Shovel. Barrow. Soil. Rubbers. Don't forget them. If you fiddle about with that Dulcie, wear a rubber. Otherwise it's tragedy time. Your thing can be your downfall. It's a man's tragedy. Our Greek tragedy. (*motioning him back to work*) Back on the chain gang.

LEWIS It's rock hard.

ERIC It needs more water. Put the hose on it.

LEWIS His hose?

ERIC Well, we're not going to go home and get ours, are we? (*Lewis picks up hose and goes to turn it on, then suddenly he spots something*)

LEWIS Dad! (*Eric looks around*) Someone at the window!

ERIC Damn!

LEWIS What'll we do?

ERIC Piss off, that's what we'll do.

LEWIS He's seen us!

ERIC Don't be a sis: he hasn't! The wheelbarrow! The wheelbarrow!

LEWIS *panicking* He's seen us.

ERIC Come on. (*They rush off with their equipment*)

Scene Five

Backyard. **Lewis**' *house. Late afternoon.* **Eric** *leading* **Norma**, *who is wearing a blindfold, out into the backyard.*

NORMA But why am I blindfolded?

ERIC A surprise.

NORMA I feel lost.

ERIC You're supposed to. (*Lewis is raking the last of the soil on the back lawn. Eric is impatient for Lewis to finish*) Hurry, Lewis. (*Lewis hurries off with his barrow and rake*)

NORMA How long do I keep this on?

ERIC Not long now. (*Eric spins Norma*)

NORMA What are you doing?

ERIC It's part of the surprise.

NORMA I'm getting giddy.

ERIC Good. (**Lewis** *comes outside and* **Eric** *stops spinning* **Norma**)

NORMA The world is turning.

ERIC It'll stop in a moment. (*he takes off the blindfold.* **Norma** *is stunned at what she sees*) Like a billiard table, isn't it?

NORMA You've levelled the lawn.

ERIC Spirit levelled.

NORMA You did it.

ERIC Me and Lewis.

NORMA It's wonderful. (*she kisses* **Lewis***, then* **Eric**) Thank you. Both of you.
(*she admires the backyard*) Where did you get the soil? 59

ERIC Manna from the sky. A miracle.

NORMA You bought it?

ERIC It was free.

NORMA Free?

ERIC You can grow anything on it. It's the best soil. Flower beds there. Vegetable garden down the back. Willow trees along the side, like you get along the Murray.

NORMA It's very black.

ERIC Rich Merri Creek soil.

NORMA Merri Creek?

ERIC Only the best for you. (*her suspicions are growing*)

NORMA Where did you keep it?

ERIC Keep what?

NORMA The soil. The stolen soil.

Eric What are you on about?

Norma I am not entirely stupid. Lewis, did you steal the soil? (**Lewis** *looks to his father for some guidance*)

Eric *to* **Lewis** Women always find it difficult to accept presents.

Norma It was you. You stole the soil from people's gardens!

Eric It's not as if we dug great big bloody quarries in every front yard. A tiny bit from here, a little from there, that's all, they hardly missed it! (*silence*)

59 **Norma** I want you to return it.

Eric You must be mad. The yard is level. Fertile.

Norma Return the soil. (*pause*)

Scene Six

Inside and outside the house.

Narrator We returned the soil. It took us a week. We filled the holes we had dug and if they had been filled in the meantime we deposited the soil near the front doors so, dad said, 'the spastics could see that their soil had been returned'. Mum and Dad didn't say another word to each other. We children passed on their messages.

Lights up on **Norma** *laying out playing cards to tell her fortune. She is in the house.*

Outside, **Eric** *is in the backyard.*

Eric *to himself.* It could have been the most perfect backyard on the whole estate. (*a beat*) Greek tragedy. That's what it is. (*he starts singing the song* Carrickfergus)

> I wished I had you in Carrickfergus
> Only for nights in Ballygrand
> I would swim over the deepest ocean
> The deepest ocean to be by your side.

And in Kilkenny it is reported
on Marble as black as ink
with gold and silver I did support her
but I'll sing no more until I get a drink.

Norma is looking at her future in the cards.

ERIC So I'll spend my days in endless roving
soft is the grass and my bed is free
Oh to be home now in Carrickfergus
on the long road down to the salty sea.

NARRATOR He always appeared singing *It's all in the game* and left
singing *Carrickfergus*. He was possessed by distance. Marriage and
children couldn't compete with that. (*a beat*) He went that
summer night saying he was going to see a friend. As we used to
say 'He went walkabout'. We got a postcard from Darwin, saying
he would be coming back once he made money working a mine.
It was the last time I saw him. He never returned. (*to **Eric***)
Where did you go after that?

ERIC Wherever you imagined I did. I went searching for Lasseter's
Reef, marlin fishing off Cape York, kangaroo shooting in Back of
Bourke, became a stock car driver, drove motorbikes through a
wall of fire, lived underground for years mining opals.

I'm drunk today and I'm rarely sober
A handsome rover from town to town.

NARRATOR We missed him.

ERIC Oh, but I am sick now and my days are numbered
Come all ye young men and lay me down.

NARRATOR We forgave him. But then, we forgive fathers
everything.

Eric vanishes.

GLOSSARY

Dialect words

Wiz – someone who is clever or good at something

Oz – Australia

sheila – woman

krauts – Germans

POWS – Prisoners of war

Commies – communists

Yankee – an American

a dago – someone from the Mediterranean, usually of Spanish extraction

a wog – western oriental gentleman (a racist term used to refer to people of colour)

smokos – cigarette break

not the full quid – not completely sane or normal

up the duff – pregnant

the slant eyes – the Japanese

a poof – an effeminate or gay man

Rubbers – condoms

a sis – short for sissy: a cowardly or effeminate boy/man

spastics – someone suffering from spasms or cerebral palsy

walkabout – a period spent in the Australian Bush by Aborigines

NOTE: many of these words are deliberately offensive within the context of the play and reflect the attitudes of the character speaking them and of many Australians in the early 1960s. They are in fact derived from British Army slang and are part of the colonial heritage of Australia.

Staging the extract

 ## SET DESIGN AND PROPS

This extract is in six short scenes. As a whole, the play has 28 short scenes. This means that the there are a lot of scene changes and it would be difficult to use an elaborate set. The play is most likely to be staged in a studio space with minimal set and prop requirements.

Read through the extract making a note of the setting of each scene and at what time it takes place.

In all the set needs to suggest **five** different locations. An effective way of achieving this is to use what is called a **composite setting** where the stage area is divided up into different areas. Each area is defined by lighting. The diagram shows one possible layout for the extract:

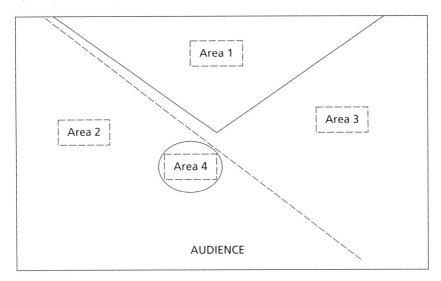

Area 1: The bedroom and the interior of the house.
Area 2: The backyard.
Area 3: The front yard of a neighbour's house.
Area 4: The underneath of the house.

For each area you will need to consider the props and lighting that will best suggest its location to an audience.

The Narrator can move freely in and out of the different areas as the whole set represents his memories, thoughts and imagination. He can be lit in one area whilst the action takes place in another.

Louis Nowra's description of the real location of the events in the play helps to give you some idea of the visual environment.

The landscape of the play is recognisably Fawkner, a suburb to the north of Melbourne. For years the only thing notable about it was that it housed the dead. Fawkner cemetery was the only thing that grew. The rest of the suburb was paddocks. There were very few trees, only long grass, cracked earth and the only colour was the purple scotch thistles in spring. In 1949 the Housing Commission built 113 houses. The experiment was a public relations disaster. The houses, constructed out of concrete blocks, may have been cheap but they had no sewerage and the roads were unmade. My family lived in one of these 113 houses, in a landscape so drab and boring that only the landscape of the mind offered colour and excitement.

◆2a Discussion

- What impression does this description give you of the location of the play?

- What colours, textures, materials and items of scenery and props might you use to create the impression given to you by this description on stage?

- How does the Housing Estate where Lewis/Louis lived compare to where you live?

LIGHTING

The use of lighting in this extract is crucial both to define the location of scenes and to indicate the time of day. The type of setting described above requires each of the four areas to be lit separately so that the audience's attention can be focused on particular areas of the stage.

How will you use lighting to define the different times of day and night and to highlight the actors' faces?

 ## COSTUMES

The costumes for this extract are everyday clothes worn in 1962, apart from the Narrator who needs to be wearing something that suggests a period some 10–20 years later. The climate is hot so the clothes are likely to be light in colour and made of fairly thin material. You will probably find clothes that look old fashioned enough in charity shops to costume the play.

Research the sort of clothes worn by Australians in the early 1960s, then go through each scene making a note of any clues to what the characters might be wearing.

Typical 1960's Australian dress, taken from a production of Summer of the Aliens.

🎵 MUSIC AND SOUND

Music in the form of songs is a central feature of this extract. Eric sings two songs that become a metaphor for his arrival and for his departure:

> "He always appeared singing *It's all in the game* and left singing *Carrickfergus*."

It is important for the actor playing Eric to know the words and music of these two songs.

It's all in the game

This is a famous 1950's American popular song. The tune, "Melody in A major" was written by a Chicago banker, Charles Dawes in 1912 and in 1951, Carl Sigman wrote a lyric that fitted the music. The song was recorded in 1951 by a number of singers but became a Number One hit in the USA and the UK when it was re-recorded by Tommy Edwards (a black singer who sounded a lot like Nat King Cole) in stereo with a rhythm and blues beat. It has become a classic love song but it is used with a sense of irony in the play because Eric almost behaves like the lover who is being sung about in the song. Lines from the song like, "Once in a while he won't call/But it's all in the game", are full of resonance when they are sung by Eric because he has not called his wife in a long time.

You can hear a MIDI file of this song at
www.discoverynet.com/~ajsnead/pre_50s/pre_50s_1.html

Carrickfergus

This is a traditional Irish folk song that has many different versions. The people that the characters in the play are based on are of Irish or Scottish descent and, according to Nowra, "had the collective memory of our ancestors". This song is part of Eric's upbringing but again he has virtually become "the handsome rover" who will spend his 'days in endless roving' as the words in the song put it. You can listen to a MIDI file of the song at **www.traditionalmusic.co.uk**

Twinkle, twinkle little star

It seems to be in Eric's nature to sing. At the start of Scene Four, he takes the first line and the tune of this famous nursery rhyme and adapts it to describe his situation:

Twinkle, twinkle little star/ Sixteen days and there you are.

Step we gaily on we go

This is a traditional Scottish folk song and dance that is also known as, *The Lewis Bridal Song*. Again, the use of the song has a purpose in that it says something about Norma's mood. The song probably reminds her of her wedding day that she associates with happy memories. Eric's return seems to have triggered her singing of this song.

All of these songs are used **diegetically**, this means that they exist within the world of the play. Non-diegetic music is music that is used to create atmosphere or to underscore the action of a play. You may want to consider using additional songs of the period to accompany the scene changes and to create an aural impression of the early 1960s for the audience. Sound effects can also be used to create atmosphere and a sense of location. Given its setting (place and time of day/night), what sound effects would be appropriate?

◆2b Sound tape

In groups

Make up a sound tape of songs from the late 50s and early 60s that you might play as the audience is entering the performance space. Also include music and sound effects to be played at appropriate moments throughout the performance.

Compare your selection with that of another group and discuss the effects of the different choices.

Exploring the extract

These extracts from *Summer of the Aliens* require four actors. The characters are a husband and wife and their son Lewis. Two actors are required to play the role of Lewis: one as the adult Narrator and the other as Lewis as a 14 year-old boy. There is obviously an age difference between the characters that can be achieved by using actors of different ages but you are likely to be working with actors of similar ages.

◆2c **Discussion**

In casting the play, you are going to have to think about two basic things:

- How are you going to show the age difference between the adults (Narrator, Norma and Eric) and the 14 year old Lewis?

- How are you going to cast the older and younger Lewis so that there is a sense of them being the same person?

HISTORICAL CONTEXT

The play is set during the Cuban Missile Crisis of 1962, at a time when the USA and Russia were hostile towards each other. Both countries had built up a huge arsenal of nuclear weapons to threaten each other with. Russia was a Communist Republic and seen by most countries in the West (which includes Australia) as an enemy of Capitalism and Democracy. The tiny island of Cuba is less than 150 miles south of the Florida coast and it is a Communist country that at the time was ruled by General Fidel Castro. (This explains the references to 'Castro's bedroom' and 'Commies' in the play). Castro allowed the Russians to establish Nuclear missile bases in Cuba which the then President of the USA (John F Kennedy), considered to be a threat to his country's security. On October 24th 1962, the USA began a naval blockage of Cuba until Kennedy persuaded President Khruschev of Russia to have the

Cuban Missiles dismantled. On November 20th 1962, the blockade of Cuba ended and the crisis was averted. A year later, on November 22nd 1963, President John F Kennedy was assassinated in Dallas, Texas.

GENRE AND SUBJECT MATTER

Summer of the Aliens is probably best described as a Memory play that uses the structure of Epic Theatre. The scenes are relatively short and the action moves rapidly from one location to another in a way that is similar to the short scenes in a film. The play was originally written for radio and adapted for the stage later and this partly accounts for the way it is written. The dialogue is mostly naturalistic in the way that the characters speak to one another. The device of a Narrator is used to create distance between the audience and the events that are happening on stage, and he speaks directly to the audience. The past world of the Narrator's imagination and the present world of him speaking to the audience come together when the Narrator speaks directly to the Eric of the past and the Eric of the past replies to the Lewis of the future.

The play is semi-autobiographical or as Louis Nowra describes it,

It is more a work of fiction with autobiographical elements. I can say that there are aspects of my own parents in Norma and Eric but in reality they were different people, just as I was, though to a lesser degree. What I have done is act like Frankenstein. Like the doctor I have raided the graveyard of my memory and have created a monster out of the various limbs and appendages I could dig up.

◆2d Raiding the graveyard of your memories

This activity is about using your own childhood memories to create a play in much the same way that Louis Nowra approached the writing of *Summer of the Aliens*.

In groups

1. Each person describes their earliest memory of their childhood whilst the rest of the group writes it down or records it on audiotape.

cont...

2. Each person then describes a further three strong memories spanning from about the age of 5 until the age of 12. These are also recorded.

3. The group now has "the various limbs and appendages" (as Nowra describes them) to create a memory play of your own. Use either the memories recorded from one person or mix and match memories from different people to write your play. The play should be about the memories of ONE fictitious character even though they may have come from different people in real life. Each person can write a scene of their own first to create the play or the group can decide to create different scenes using improvisation. You can use ideas from *Summer of the Aliens* to structure your play, like the use of a **Narrator** and **cross-cutting** between different locations in short scenes.

4. After rehearsal each group performs their memory play to the class. Take part in a Critic's Forum after the performance of each play and note down the views and opinions that are expressed about the performances under discussion.

5. Use your notes to write your own critical review of the performances you have seen and the performance you have taken part in.

◆2e Hot-seating

One of the main issues in this extract is the responsibility of **ERIC** as a parent and as a father. The events revolve around the fact that Eric has been away, turns up out of the blue and goes away again.

A volunteer takes on the role of Eric to answer questions put to him about his actions, motives and feelings. The person in the 'hot-seat' must answer in role as Eric would have. The purpose of the exercise is to try to understand the character's real feelings and motives in the extract.

Discuss and evaluate the answers given, then repeat the exercise with someone in the role of Norma in the 'hot-seat', followed by Lewis at 14, followed by the older Lewis.

◆2f Discussion and critical writing

Discuss the following, either in groups or as a class, then use the points raised for a piece of critical writing in which you discuss what qualities you would expect to find in the ideal parents.

- How does Eric match your ideas of what a father should or could be?
- How does Norma match your ideas of what a mother should or could be?
- To what extent do Norma and Eric compare with your experience of your own mother and father or other people's mothers or fathers?
- How does the older Lewis (the Narrator) think differently about his father's behaviour than the younger Lewis?
- How do you think Norma feels about her husband's behaviour? Is she in any way responsible for the way he behaves?
- The Narrator says: "we forgive fathers everything." Would you forgive your father everything?

Exploring characters

ERIC

♦2g Role play

This is a role-play scenario aimed at exploring the beliefs, attitudes and values held by someone like Eric.

In groups

Organisation: The scene takes place in **one** of the following: a café, a waiting room, a train carriage, a pub. One person plays Eric who seems to have little or no respect for anyone who is not white, heterosexual male or Australian. Add one or more of the following roles: a working mother; a refugee; a teacher; a single parent; a social worker; a student; a business woman; a passenger; a customer.

Situation: Eric is reading a newspaper. He reads out the following headline:

Australia to take in 20,000 refugees.

The scene begins with Eric's response to this headline spoken out loud. The other character(s) must challenge any racist or sexist remarks made by Eric. Your aim is to try and change the way Eric thinks and feels about women and non-white Australians in particular without resorting to either physical violence or verbal abuse.

Opening line: ERIC   Not another load of dagos moving here, taking all our jobs and all our houses...

Evaluate the different groups' performances that you see.

♦2h Further discussion

- Where do attitudes like those expressed by Eric come from?
- To what extent can you change an individual's attitudes and behaviour?

◆2i **Still images and thought-tracking**

Still image is a useful technique to use when exploring, amongst other things, the ways in which the spatial relationships (or proxemics) between characters communicate a particular meaning to an audience. **Thought-tracking** is a technique that helps to explore the sub-text of a play. The sub-text is what is going on beneath the words; in other words it is a way of exploring the hidden meanings in a play. Thought-tracking can be used as part of a still image exercise. During the still image, each of the participants is tapped on the shoulder and asked what they are thinking and feeling about the situation at that moment or about one of the other characters in the still image. The person whose shoulder is tapped speaks the thoughts of the character at that moment in time.

In groups
Create still images that depict the following episodes from the extract.

1. Eric's return after three years.
Key line – **Narrator:** We children were glad to have him home, unlike my grandmother and, of course, my mother. **37**

2. Eric and Norma arguing about why he went away and Lewis listening in the doorway.
Key line – **Norma:** What are you doing up at this hour, love? **39**

3. Eric and Lewis under the house with Norma singing and dancing overhead.
Key line – **Eric:** Bit of a bounce in her footsteps. Probably thinking of me. **41**

4. Eric and Lewis shovelling soil into a wheelbarrow.
Key line – **Narrator:** So over the following night we stole soil from our neighbours' front yards. **43**

5. Eric and Lewis are nearly caught.
Key line – **Lewis:** Dad! Someone at the window! **44**

6. Taking the blindfold off Norma and seeing the newly levelled lawn.
Key line – **Norma:** It's wonderful. Thank you. Both of you. **45**

7. Norma tells them to take back the soil.
Key line – **Norma:** I want you to return it. **46**

8. Eric leaves for the final time.
Key line – **Narrator:** He went walkabout. *cont...* **47**

What does this exercise reveal to you about the body language of the characters?

How have the inner thoughts of the characters deepened your understanding of them?

◆2j Narration

Consider the sequence of events that happen in the play and write your own narration for the extract. Instead of the older Lewis narrating the story, choose either Norma or Eric to tell the story and write a Narration from their point of view.

Perform your Narration to the rest of the class or have someone else perform it for you.

What does your new Narration reveal about any of the characters? What do other people's Narration sequences that you have watched reveal about the characters?

COMPARING TEXTS

◆2k Themes for Comparison: Absent fathers and duty

- Both Lewis in *Summer of the Aliens* and Lucas in *Loon Boy* come from unstable family backgrounds. Lewis grows up only seeing and knowing his father for two short periods in his life, whilst Lucas has never known his father. What effects does this have on the boys in these two plays? What do the plays tell you about the relationship between parents and children?

- Eric has a duty to his wife and children in *Summer of the Aliens* and Anowa has a duty to her mother and father. In each play these characters are seen as not fulfilling their duty to their respective family. What constitutes the sense of duty in each play and how does it compare to any sense of duty you feel you may have to your own family?

Anowa

Ama Ata Aidoo

AMA ATA AIDOO

Ama Ata Aidoo was born in the small town of Abeadzi Kyiakor, in 1942 when Ghana was known by its colonial name, The Gold Coast. Her father was one of the village chiefs and she was brought up in the royal household. At the age of 15, Ama Ata Aidoo, decided she wanted to become a writer and by the age of 19 she had won a prize for a short story in a newspaper competition. From 1961 to 1964, she attended the University of Ghana at Legon and her first play, *The Dilemma of a Ghost*, was produced there in 1964. As well as being a writer and critic, Ama Ata Aidoo has been a teacher and lecturer in both Africa and the USA and a politician. In January 1982, Aidoo was Minister of Education in Ghana but resigned after 18 months feeling unable to achieve her aim of making education in Ghana freely accessible to all. To date she has written two plays, two novels (*Changes* won the Commonwealth Writers Prize for best book in 1992), a collection of short stories, two collection of poetry and numerous essays on African literature and the status of women in African society.

SUMMARY OF THE PLOT

The play is based on a traditional Ghanaian folk-tale, which deals with the story of a handsome stranger who enters a village, carries off the most beautiful girl and eventually destroys her. Anowa in the play is a 'free-spirit' who wants to be a dancing priestess but her mother, Badua, will not allow it and wants her to marry a man of their choosing. Anowa falls in love with Kofi Ako and marries him against her parents' wishes. Anowa and Kofi leave for the coast to make their fortune, but their love for one another begins to fade, as Kofi Ako becomes involved in the Slave trade much against Anowa's wishes. Anowa resents being told that she does not have to work because they have slaves to do the work. She is morally outraged that her husband has become as bad as the white foreign traders. Kofi tries to banish Anowa but she publicly humiliates him by saying that he has been unable to give her children. Kofi cannot bear the shame of his manhood being brought into question and he shoots himself. Anowa finds herself totally alone without her husband and with no family to turn to so she drowns herself.

The story of the play is told by an Old Man and an Old Woman, known as *The-Mouth-That-Eats-Salt-And-Pepper* and they act as commentators on the action.

THE CONTEXT OF THE SCENE

This extract is the first dialogue scene from the play when Anowa arrives home to tell her mother and father that she has found a husband.

Anowa

By

Ama Ata Aidoo – Ghana, West Africa (1970)

CAST LIST

ANOWA – a young woman
BADUA – her mother who complains at the beginning and cries at the end
OSAM – her father who smokes his pipe

Setting

In Yebi. 1870s.

*Upper stage. The courtyard of **Maami Badua** and **Papa Osram**'s cottage. Village noises. Standing in the centre is an earthen hearth with tripod cooking pot. There are a couple of small household stools standing around. By the right wall is a lie-in chair that belongs exclusively to **Papa OSAM**. Whenever he sits down, he sits in this. By the chair is a small table. The lower stage here represents a section of a village street from which there is an open entrance into the courtyard. In the background, upper left and upper right, there are doors connecting the courtyard to the inner rooms of the house. In the pot something is cooking which, throughout the scene, **Maami Badua** will go and stir. By the hearth is a small vessel into which she puts the ladle after each stirring. **Badua** enters from upper right, goes to the hearth, picks up the ladle and stirs the soup. She is talking loudly to herself.*

BADUA Any mother would be concerned if her daughter refused to get married six years after her puberty. If I do not worry about this, what shall I worry about?

Osam enters from upper left smoking his pipe.

BADUA Besides, a woman is not a stone but a human being; she grows.

OSAM Woman, (**Badua** *turns to look at him*) that does not mean you should break my ears with your complaints. (*he looks very composed*)

BADUA What did you say, Osam?

OSAM I say you complain too much. (*he goes to occupy the lie in chair, and exclaims, 'Ah!' with satisfaction*)

BADUA *seriously* Are you trying to send me insane?

OSAM Will that shut you up?

BADUA Kofi Sam! (*now she really is angry*)

OSAM Yes, my wife.

(*Badua breathes audibly with exasperation. She begins pacing up and down the courtyard, with the ladle in her hand.*)

BADUA *moving quickly up to* **Osam** So it is nothing at a-a-l-l (*stretching the utterance of the last word*) to you that your child is not married and goes round wild, making everyone talk about her?

OSAM Which is your headache, that she is not yet married, or that she is wild?

BADUA Hmm!

OSAM You know that I am a man and getting daughters married is not one of my duties. Getting them born, aha! But not finding them husbands.

BADUA Hmm! (*paces up and down*)

OSAM And may the ancestral spirits help me, but what man would I order from the heavens to please the difficult eye of my daughter Anowa?

BADUA Hmm! (*she goes and stirs the soup and this time remembers to put the ladle down. She stands musing by the hearth*)

Osam As for her wildness, what do you want me to say again about that? I have always asked you to apprentice her to a priestess to quieten her down. But …

*(roused again, **Badua** moves quickly back to where he is and meanwhile, corks both her ears with two fingers and shakes her head to make sure he notices what she is doing)*

Osam *chuckles* Hmm, play children's games with me, my wife. One day you will click your fingers and regret that you did not listen to me.

Badua *removers her fingers from her ears* I have said it and I will say it again and again and again! I am not going to turn my only daughter into a dancer priestess.

Osam What is wrong with priestesses?

Badua I don't say there is anything wrong with them.

Osam Did you not consult them over and over again when you could not get a single child from your womb to live beyond one day?

Badua *reflectively* O yes. I respect them, I honour them … I fear them. Yes, my husband, I fear them. But my only daughter shall not be a priestess.

Osam They have so much glory and dignity…

Badua But in the end, they are not people. They become too much like the gods they interpret.

As she enumerates the attributes of priesthood, her voice grows hysterical and her face terror-stricken. **Osam** *removes his pipe, and stares at her, his mouth open with amazement.*

Badua They counsel with spirits;
They read into other men's souls;
They swallow dogs' eyes
Jump fires
Drink goats' blood

80

Sheep milk
Without flinching
Or vomiting
They do not feel
As you or I,
They have no shame.

(she relaxes, and **Osam** *does too, the latter sighing audibly.* **Badua**
continues, her face slightly turned away from both her husband and the
audience)

I want my child
To be a human woman
Marry a man,
Tend a farm
And be happy to see her.
Peppers and her onions grow.
A woman like her
Should bear children
Many children,
So she can afford to have
One or two die.
Should she not take
Her place at meetings
Among the men and women of the clan?
And sit on my chair when
I am gone? And a captainship in the army,
Should not be beyond her
When the time is ripe.

Osam *nods his head and exclaims,* 'Oh … oh!'

Badua But a priestess lives too much in her own and other
people's minds, my husband.

Osam *sighing again* My wife, people with better vision than yours or
mine have seen that Anowa is not like you or me. And a prophet
with a locked mouth is neither a prophet nor a man. Besides, the
yam that will burn, shall burn, boiled or roasted.

Badua *picks up the ladle but does not stir the pot. Throws her arms about*
Since you want to see Nkomfo and Nsofo, seers and dancers…

ANOWA *from the distance* Mother!

BADUA That is her coming.

ANOWA Father!

OSAM O yes. Well let us keep quiet about her affairs then. You know what heart lies in her chest.

ANOWA Mother, Father ... Father, Mother ... Mother ...

*Osam jumps up and confused, he and **Badua** keep bumping into each other as each moves without knowing why or where he or she is moving. **Badua** still has the ladle in her hands.*

BADUA Why do you keep hitting at me?

ANOWA Mother!

OSAM Sorry, I did not mean to. But you watch your step too.

ANOWA Father!

OSAM And where is she?

Anowa runs in, lower right, with her empty water-pot.

BADUA Hei. Why do you frighten me so? And where is the water?

ANOWA O Mother. *(she stops running and stays on the lower stage)*

OSAM What is it?

ANOWA *her eyes swerving from the face of one to the other* O Father!

OSAM Say whatever you have got to say and stop behaving like a child.

BADUA Calling us from the street!

OSAM What have you got to tell us that couldn't wait until you reached here?

ANOWA O Father.

BADUA And look at her. See here, it is time you realised you have grown up.

ANOWA Mother … (*moving a step or two forward*)

BADUA And now what is it? Besides, where is the water? I am sure this household will go to bed to count the beams tonight since there is no water to cook with.

ANOWA Mother, Father, I have met the man I want to marry.

BADUA What is she saying?

ANOWA I say I have found the man I would like to marry.

BADUA & OSAM Eh?

Long pause during which **Badua** *stares at* **Anowa** *with her head tilted to one side.*

ANOWA Kofi Ako asked me to marry him and I said I will, too.

BADUA Eh?

OSAM Eh?

BADUA Eh?

OSAM Eh?

BADUA Eh?

OSAM & BADUA Eh – eh!

79 *Light dies on all three and comes up again almost immediately.* **Osam** *is sitting in his chair.* **Anowa** *hovers around and she has a chewing stick in her mouth with which she scrapes her teeth when she is not speaking.* **Badua** *is sitting by the hearth doing nothing.*

ANOWA Mother, you have been at me for a long time to get married. And now that I have found someone I like very much …

83 **BADUA** Anowa, shut up. Shut up! Push your tongue into your mouth and close it. Shut up because I never counted Kofi Ako

68

among my sons-in-law. Anowa, why Kofi Ako? Of all the
mothers that are here in Yebi, should I be the one whose
daughter would want to marry this fool, this good-for-nothing
cassava-man, this watery male of all watery males? This-I-am-
the-handsome-one-with-a-stick-between-my-teeth-in-the-
market-place… This… this…

ANOWA O Mother…

BADUA *quietly* I say Anowa, why did you not wait for a day when I
was cooking banku and your father was drinking palm-wine in
the market place with his friends? When you could have
snatched the ladle from my hands and hit me with it and taken
your father's wine from his hands and thrown it into his face?
Anowa, why did you not wait for a day like that, since you want
to behave like the girl in the folk-tale?

ANOWA But what are you talking about, Mother?

BADUA And you, Kobina Sam, will you not say anything?

OSAM Abena Badua, leave me out of this. You know that if I so
much as whisper anything to do with Anowa, you and your
brothers and your uncles will tell me to go and straighten out the
lives of my nieces. This is your family drum; beat it, my wife.

BADUA I did not ask you for riddles.

OSAM Mm… just remember I was smoking my pipe.

BADUA If you had been any other father, you would have known
what to do and what not to do.

OSAM Perhaps; but that does not mean I would have done
anything. The way you used to talk, I thought if Anowa came to
tell you she was going to get married to Kweku Ananse, or
indeed the devil himself, you would spread rich cloth before her
to walk on. And probably sacrifice an elephant.

BADUA And do you know what this Kofi Ako is like?

ANOWA What is he like?

BADUA My lady, I have not asked you a question.

Anowa retires into sullenness. She scrapes her teeth noisily.

OSAM How would I know what he is like? Does he not come from Nsona House? And is not that one of the best Houses that are here in Yebi? Has he an ancestor who unclothed himself to nakedness, had the Unmentionable, killed himself or another man?

BADUA And if all that there is to a young man is that his family has had an unspoiled name, then what kind of a man is he? Are he and his wife going to feed on stones when he will not put a blow into a thicket or at least learn a trade?

OSAM Anyway, I said long ago that I was removing my mouth from my daughter Anowa's marriage. Did I not say that? She would not allow herself to be married to any man who came to ask for her hand from us and of whom we approved. Did you not know then that when she chose a man, it might be one of whom we would disapprove?

BADUA But why should she want to do a thing like that?

OSAM My wife, do remember I am a man, the son of a woman who also has five sisters. It is a long time since I gave up trying to understand the human female. Besides, if you think well of it, I am not the one to decide finally whom Anowa can marry. Her uncle, your brother is there, is he not? You'd better consult him. Because I know your family: they will say I deliberately married Anowa to a fool to spite them.

ANOWA Father, Kofi Ako is not a fool.

OSAM My daughter, please forgive me, I am sure you know him very well. And it was only by way of speaking. Kwame! Kwame! I thought the boy was around somewhere. (*moves towards lower stage and looks around*)

BADUA What are you calling him for?

OSAM To go and call us her uncle and your brother.

BADUA Could we not have waited until this evening or dawn tomorrow?

OSAM For what shall we wait for the dawn?

BADUA To settle the case.

OSAM What case? Who says I want to settle cases? If there is any case to settle, that is between you and your people. It is not everything one chooses to forget, Badua. Certainly, I remember what happened in connection with Anowa's dancing. That is, if you don't. Did they not say in the end that it was I who had prevented her from going into apprenticeship with a priestess?

Light dies down on them and comes on a little later. **Anowa** *is seen dressed in a two-piece cloth. She darts in and out of upper right, with very quick movements. She is packing her belongings into a little basket. Every now and then, she pauses, looks at her mother and sucks her teeth.* **Badua** *sits by the hearth complaining tearfully.* **Osam** *is lying in his chair smoking.* 79

BADUA I am in disgrace so suck your teeth at me. *(silence)* Other women certainly have happier tales to tell about motherhood. *(silence)* I think I am just an unlucky woman.

ANOWA Mother, I do not know what is wrong with you.

BADUA And how would you know what is wrong with me? Look here Anowa, marriage is like a piece of cloth… 83

ANOWA I like mine and it is none of your business.

BADUA And like cloth, its beauty passes with wear and tear.

ANOWA I do not care, Mother. Have I not told you that this is to be my marriage and not yours?

BADUA My marriage! Why should it be my daughter who would want to marry that good-for-nothing cassava-man?

ANOWA He is mine and I like him.

BADUA If you like him, do like him. The men of his house do not make good husbands; ask older women who are married to Nsona man.

OSAM You know what you are saying is not true. Indeed from the beginning of time Nsona men have been known to make the best of husbands.

Badua *glares at him*

ANOWA That does not even worry me and it should not worry you, Mother.

BADUA It's up to you, my mistress who knows everything. But remember, my lady – when I am too old to move, I shall be sitting by these walls waiting for you to come back with your rags and nakedness.

ANOWA You do not have to wait because we shall not be coming back here to Yebi. Not for a long long time, Mother, not for a long long time.

BADUA Of course, if I were you I wouldn't want to come back with my shame either.

ANOWA You will be surprised to know that I am going to help him do something with his life.

BADUA A-a-h, I wish I could turn into a bird and come and stand on your roof-top watching you make something of that husband of yours. What was he able to make of the plantation of palm-trees his grandfather gave him? And the virgin land his uncles gave him, what did he do with that?

ANOWA Please, Mother, remove your witch's mouth from our marriage.

Osam *jumps up and from now on hovers between the two, trying to make peace*

OSAM Hei Anowa, what is wrong with you? Are you mad? How can you speak like that to your mother?

ANOWA But Father, Mother does not treat me like her daughter.

BADUA And so you call me a witch? The thing is, I wish I were a witch so that I could protect you from your folly.

ANOWA I do not need your protection, Mother.

OSAM The spirits of my fathers! Anowa, what daughter talks like this to her mother?

ANOWA But Father, what mother talks to her daughter the way Mother talks to me? And now, Mother, I am going, so take your witchery to eat in the sea.

OSAM Ei Anowa?

BADUA Thank you my daughter .

Badua & Anowa try to jump on each other. Baduu attempts to hit Anowa but Osam quickly intervenes.

OSAM What has come over this household? Tell me what has come over this household? And you too Badua. What has come over you?

BADUA You leave me alone, Osam. Why don't you speak to Anowa? She is your daughter, I am not.

OSAM Well, she is not mature.

BADUA That one makes me laugh. Who is not mature? Has she not been mature enough to divine me out and discover I am a witch? Did she not choose her husband single-handed? And isn't she leaving home to make a better success of her marriage?

OSAM Anowa, have you made up your mind to leave?

ANOWA But Father, Mother is driving me away.

BADUA Who is driving you away?

ANOWA You! Who does not know here in Yebi that from the day I came to tell you that Kofi and I were getting married you have been drumming into my ears what a disgrace this marriage is going to be for you? Didn't you say that your friends were laughing at you? And they were saying that very soon I shall be sharing your clothes because my husband will never buy me any? Father, I am leaving this place.

She picks up her basket, puts it on her head and moves down towards lower left.

BADUA Yes, go.

ANOWA I am on my way, Mother.

OSAM And where is your husband?

ANOWA I am going to look for him.

OSAM Anowa, stop!

*But **Anowa** behaves as if she has not heard him*

OSAM Anowa, you must not leave in this manner.

BADUA Let her go. And may she walk well.

ANOWA Mother, I shall walk so well that I will not find my feet back here again.

*She exits lower left. **Osam** spits with disdain, then stares at **Badua** for a long time. She slowly bows her head in the folds of her cloth and begins to weep quietly as the lights die on them.*

GLOSSARY

Yam – an important food similar to the potato in West Africa. Yams can be boiled, fried, baked or roasted. Boiled Yams are pounded into a pulp to make thick dough called *fufu* that is eaten with soups.

Cassava-man – someone who farms the cassava plant, which is a staple food in West Africa. It too is used to make *fufu*. It grows well in wet or dry climates and requires very little work to make it grow. Badua is therefore suggesting that Kofi is lazy.

Banku – a favourite Ghanaian food made from corn that has been pounded and cooked into a paste. It is served with a thick spicy soup or sauce.

Kweku Ananse – a spider that appears in a number of Ghanaian folk tales. He is portrayed as a troublemaker and plays tricks on people.

Kwame; Kofi – most African names are chosen for their meaning. Kwame is a name given to male children born on a Saturday and Kofi is a name given to a male child born on a Friday.

The Unmentionable – a sexually transmitted disease such as syphilis.

Staging the extract

SET DESIGN AND PROPS

The setting for this extract can be very simple. The playwright suggests the use of an upper stage to represent the courtyard of the house and a lower stage to represent the street, but this extract can take place in one space as the action is all in the courtyard.

Go through the extract listing all of the properties required and find a picture to accompany each of the items.

LIGHTING

This extract is split into three scenes that are indicated by lighting changes. Lighting can be used to create a sense of a hot climate either by the use of intense spotlights or by tinting the lighting with gold and yellow.

COSTUMES

The author suggests that for costume, "anything African will do as long as a certain consistency is followed." Look at some traditional Ghanaian designs for costume material and the ways in which the women wear their clothes. You could obtain some material of your own and experiment with different ways of wrapping it around yourself.

MUSIC AND SOUND

Music is an important feature in the play and helps to locate it culturally. The Atenteben is a wind instrument and the sound is used to symbolise Anowa. The Bull's Horn and the Fontonfrom are other African instruments that might be used in the play. Identify some traditional African instruments and listen to recordings of them. You may want to use some music at the beginning and end of the play and some snippets of music in the two scene changes.

To create the atmosphere of an African village you can create a soundscape that can be played quietly in the background during the scenes. The playwright suggests sounds like *the pounding of fufu or millet, a goat bleating loudly, a woman calling her child.*

A modern-day Ghanian woman preparing a simple meal.

Exploring the extract

HISTORICAL CONTEXT

The play is set in the 1870s when Ghana was a British colony following a British invasion in 1874. The playwright therefore creates an atmosphere of a people being enslaved to another country. But it is also provides the playwright with a context in which to question the way in which some Black Africans in the past were actually profiting from the Slave Trade.

GENRE AND SUBJECT MATTER

Anowa is a play that mixes traditional African storytelling techniques with the conventions of European theatre. The play is non-naturalistic in form in that it uses storytellers that act as both narrators and chorus to introduce and comment on the dialogue scenes. The dialogue is a mixture of ordinary spoken language, poetic phrases and stylised expression. Sections of the play are told in movement without dialogue and there are moments of ceremonial dancing accompanied by music.

The play requires an acting style that is emotionally charged and physically expressive as the characters are not afraid of showing what they think and feel. There is little need for subtlety in the acting as the character's reactions to each other are very immediate.

The extract is a continuous scene from the play, but it is broken up by two section breaks that act as jumps forward in time. The end of the first section marks the moment when Anowa breaks the news that she is marrying Kofi Ako and her parents' reaction to it. The action at this point is like a **freeze-frame**, the actors then move into new positions to take up a new freeze-frame that depicts Osam sitting in his chair, Badua sitting by the hearth and Anowa hovering around and the action and dialogue start slightly further on in time. *(Light dies on all three and comes on again almost immediately.)* The second section ends when Osam decides to involve his brother-in-law in the dispute because he feels that they will blame him for Anowa's decision to marry Kofi Ako anyway. There is a much longer jump in time at this point because something has happened or been said to make Anowa decide to pack her belongings. *(Light dies on them and comes on a little later.)*

◆3a Marking the moment

In groups

Create a **freeze-frame** for each of the moments that occur either side of the two section breaks. Learn the following lines of dialogue and present this and your freeze-frames to an audience giving each one a title or a caption.

68, 71

ANOWA Kofi Ako asked me to marry him and I said I will, too.

BADUA Eh?

OSAM Eh?

BADUA Eh?

OSAM Eh?

BADUA Eh?

OSAM & BADUA Eh – eh!

- Freeze-frame 1 with title or caption followed by
- Freeze-frame 2 with title or caption.

OSAM Who says I want to settle cases? If there is any case to settle, that is between you and your people. It is not everything one chooses to forget, Badua. Certainly, I remember what happened in connection with Anowa's dancing. That is, if you don't. Did they not say in the end that it was I who had prevented her from going into apprenticeship with a priestess?

- Freeze-frame 3 with title or caption followed by
- Freeze-frame 4 with title or caption.

BADUA I am in disgrace so suck your teeth at me.

Use one or more of the following methods to announce each of your titles or captions that will mark these moments in the play:

- speak the title or caption as a group
- use a narrator to announce each title or caption
- write the titles or captions on an overhead transparency and project them
- produce the titles on a computer and use a digital projector to project them.

How does 'marking the moment' help illustrate the changes that occur between the different sections?

◆3b **Acting**

65

Locate the speech in which Badua lists what she thinks Priests do.

How are you going to build up the hysteria in your voice during the speech?

What would make you express terror in your face as you act out the speech?

◆3c **Discussion**

In this extract Anowa is going against the cultural traditions and her parents by refusing to marry any of the men whom her parents have approved as possible husbands for her. Instead she has chosen a husband herself. It is because her parents cannot accept Kofi Ako as a son-in-law that Anowa packs her basket and leaves home for good.

- To what extent do you think parents should influence your choice of boyfriend or girlfriend?
- How do the ways in which Anowa's mother and father handle the situation differ in this extract? How might they have acted differently?

Read through the extract and list the five reasons that Badua gives for saying that Kofi Ako will not make a good husband for Anowa.

- What sort of arguments is Badua using to dismiss Kofi Ako as a possible husband for her daughter?
- Are any of the reasons she gives valid or reasonable?
- Why does Anowa not accept any of these reasons?
- What four reasons does Anowa give her parents for wanting to marry him? How are any of these reasons similar or different to that of her mother's?

◆3d **Role-play**

This role-play mirrors the circumstances of the characters in the extract. The dramatic tension in this scene is created by the fact that Anowa is determined to leave home and marry the man of her choice, whilst Badua is telling her that she is making a big mistake. Osam is acting as referee between the two of them.

In threes

Organisation: Character One (the Anowa equivalent) is right in their view; Character Two (the Badua equivalent) is right in their opposing and/or different view; Character Three (the Osam equivalent) can see both points of view.

Situation: **Either**

— a parent telling a son or daughter to eat something that they do not want to eat

or

— a parent telling a son or daughter that they are going to visit a relation that they do not get on with

The role-play continues until one of the characters leaves the room.

Evaluation: Analyse the sorts of arguments the different roles were using to justify their position. How did it feel to be the one in the middle? What light does it reflect on the position of the characters in the extract?

Repeat: This time use the scenario of the extract to role-play the scene.

Now enact the scene using the script and apply the same feelings, reactions, actions and emotions that were generated in the role-play. Experiment with taking on different roles and evaluate one another's interpretations of those roles.

Exploring characters

ANOWA

Look at Anowa's opening speeches in the first scene of the extract up until when she says, '*Kofi Ako asked me to marry him and I said I will, too*'

You will notice that Anowa says very little during her entrance other than saying 'Mother' and 'Father'. What does this tell you about her mood and the way in which she comes on stage?

♦3e Drama techniques: Thought Tunnel

This exercise is aimed at putting ideas into the head of the actor playing the character of Anowa so that they enter the scene being able to feel and communicate the mood.

In groups/as a class

The group makes two straight lines and stand facing one another to create a tunnel that the actor playing Anowa can walk through with people on each side. Anowa stands at one end on the tunnel with someone in the role of Kofi Ako and two people representing her mother and father stand at the other end of the tunnel.

The exercise begins with Kofi saying to Anowa: 'Anowa, will you marry me?' Anowa then begins her journey through the Thought Tunnel towards her parents. As she passes each person along the lines they speak a thought that might be in her head that reflects the way she is feeling. She listens to the thought and expresses her inner feelings by calling out either, 'Mother' or 'Father'. Here are some of the thoughts that people in the Thought Tunnel might say:

– I can't wait to tell mother and father the good news.

> — The handsome Kofi is going to be my husband.
>
> — I feel like my heart is going to burst.
>
> When Anowa has passed through the Thought Tunnel, she arrives to face her parents and says, "Mother, Father, I have met the man I want to marry." Badua and Osam complete the exercise by exclaiming, 'Eh!'
>
> You will need to repeat the exercise several times so that you can really build up the thoughts inside Anowa's head.

◆3f What daughter talks like this?

> Look at the scene between Osam and Badua before Anowa's entrance. Note down all the things that are said about Anowa by her Mother and Father. What sort of impression does this create about Anowa before she comes on stage?
>
> In the second section of the extract, Anowa says very little while Badua and Osam talk about her and argue with each other. What is Anowa thinking and doing throughout this scene?
>
> In the third section of the extract, Anowa behaves in a very different way than in the earlier sections of the extract. Note down the things she says and does in this section. What has caused her to behave in this way? How does the Anowa we see in this section compare to the impression created of her by Badua and Osam in the first section? How reasonable do you think her behaviour is in this section?

63–66

68–71

71–74

◆3g Letter home

H

> Imagine that you are Anowa and that it is some time since you left Yebi. You have been married to Kofi Ako for nearly two years but still haven't had any children. Some of the things that Badua warned you about Kofi Ako have come true. Write a letter in role to Badua and Osam looking back at what happened the day that you left home and what was said between you.

BADUA

Anowa's decision to marry Kofi Ako against her mother's wishes provides the dramatic tension in the scene. If Anowa had decided to stay and not marry Kofi Ako the play might have turned out quite differently. However, one of the reasons why Anowa leaves is because of the attitude of her mother.

◆3h **Forum theatre**

This exercise is aimed at exploring Badua's behaviour to see what would happen if she altered the way she behaves and speaks to Anowa.

As a class

Organisation: The group sits in a large circle. Three volunteers go into the centre of the circle and take on the roles of Badua, Osam and Anowa. The three performers begin an improvisation based on the situation in the extract.

Situation: In this improvised version of the play, you are going to attempt to stop Anowa from leaning home.

Opening line: **BADUA** You are not marrying that good for nothing cassava-man and that's final.

At any point in the improvisation, one of the performers can stop the action and ask the rest of the group who are sitting around in the circle (The Forum) for help or advice about what to do or say next. You can continue the improvisation from the point of interruption or start it again at any point you decide. Equally, anyone from the circle can stop the improvisation if they think any of the characters is saying or doing anything that is inappropriate or unhelpful. However, if you stop the improvisation you must either be prepared to go into the centre of the circle and take over one of the roles yourself or make positive suggestions to the performers about what they might say or do differently. You have to be able to tell the performers where you want the improvisation to start from again. The improvisation continues until Badua and Osam have managed to find a way of enabling Anowa to stay at home with them.

What does this exercise tell you about the way Badua behaves in the extract and the sort of person she is?

◆3i I want my child …

Locate the speech made by Badua that describes the future she sees for her daughter, beginning, "I want my child…".

How would you feel if this were the kind of future that your parents had in mind for you? If you were to have children in the future, what kind of future would you imagine for them as a parent?

66

◆3j Hopes and dreams

Write a similar speech for Anowa that begins, "I want to," in which you can capture your ideas for how Anowa imagines her future. Compare this with Badua's speech. How do they differ in the way in which they see the life ahead for Anowa? In what ways does this help to explain the animosity between mother and daughter?

H

OSAM

◆3k Drama techniques: Character collage

On your own

1. Write a list of 4 or 5 words or phrases that you think describe Osam's character throughout the extract.

2. Against each word or phrase write one line from the extract that you think supports and illustrates your description. For example, you could describe Osam as a man who thinks it is a woman's place to bring up children and use the following line to illustrate this view:

    OSAM You know that I am a man and getting daughters married is not one of my duties.

    cont…

As a group

1. Select at least six different lines from the lines provided by members of the group. Again, try and select the lines so that they are from right across the extract and that show the different aspects of Osam's character.

2. You are going to act out each of the lines in the manner that has been described in the lists you have made. Each member of the group can act out a line individually or you can present the lines as a group chorus. Each group presents their "Osam character collage" to the whole class.

3. Evaluation: what does each group's character collage tell you about Osam's character in the play?

♦31 The Agony Chat Show

Organisation: For this improvisation you will need the chat show host (you could ask your teacher to play this role); a mother and father whose daughter left home some five years ago to marry against their wishes (similar to Badua and Osam); the daughter (an Anowa equivalent) and the studio audience.

Situation: The improvisation follows the format of a television 'agony chat show'. The Host introduces his or her guests to the audience, outlining what has happened to them in the past and that they would like to see their daughter back. Their daughter is waiting secretly off stage and the parents do not know that she is there. What happens when the lost daughter is revealed?

Evaluation: What does this improvisation tell you about the situation and the characters in the play?

By the end of the scene, Osam says that he cannot understand what has come over his wife but that can make allowances for Anowa's behaviour because she is not mature. He makes a half-hearted attempt to stop her leaving at the end of the scene following the family conflict.

♦3m Script writing

Script writing 1

Imagine that the lights come up again on Osam and Badua at the end of the extract and it is five minutes later after Anowa has left. Write the scene that might go on between them.

Script writing 2

The scene changes to another part of the village. Anowa is waiting for Kofi Ako. Osam enters and is relieved to find Anowa. Write the dialogue for this scene in which Osam tries to persuade Anowa to come home.

COMPARING TEXTS – CULTURE AND SOCIETY

♦3n Cultural attitudes and markers

- Anowa and The Government Inspector, both deal with the issues of daughters leaving home to get married. How is the parents' attitude to marriage different in these two plays? Would you expect your own parents to behave like the parents in these two plays?

- Props in Anowa like the earthen hearth and Anowa's water-pot indicate the location and something about the cultural climate of the play. In other words they create an African-ness about the play. Which props, costumes and/or sound effects might achieve the same effect for the other three plays in this collection? Justify your selection of items.

Loon Boy

Kathleen McDonnell

This is what the playwright says about herself on her own web site: kathleenmcdonnell.com.

I was born in Chicago, Illinois into a large Irish-Catholic family and moved to Canada more than three decades ago. I've become a Canadian citizen but retain my American citizenship as well. Since graduating with a B.A. from the University of Toronto, I've spent most of my adult life making my living as a writer.

I make my home on Toronto Island with my partner Alec and our two daughters. The Island is a vibrant and unique place – a (mostly) car-free community a 10-minute ferry ride from downtown Toronto.

I write novels and plays for young people, as well as books and articles about kids today. In a nutshell, I write for and about kids – **for** because – to echo C.S. Lewis – I find that children's stories are usually the best medium to express what I want to say; and **about** because I have a burning interest in kids and their culture, how they think and feel about the world they're growing up in.

Kathleen McDonnell's latest book about children, *Honey, we lost the kids*, was published in September 2001. The book looks at the impact of the multimedia age on parents and their children. Her most recent plays for children include *The Seven Ravens* (2001) based on a fairy story by the Brothers Grimm, *Foundlings* (2001) set in ancient Greece, *Right of Passage* (2000) a large-scale outdoor theatre event and *Ezzie's Emerald*

(1995) a musical version of her own novel about an overweight girl and her comical fairy godmother. *Loon Boy* won the 1994 Chalmers Canadian Children's Play Award after it was first produced by the Carousel Players in Ontario Canada in 1993.

SUMMARY OF THE PLOT

Ruby's husband, Alf, has recently died and she has gone to spend some time at their lakeside home where they used to spend their summers together. Ruby used to take in foster children but has retired from it because she thought she was getting too old. Susan is a social worker who comes to Ruby with a problem. Susan has found a special group home for a really difficult child called Lucas, but she needs somewhere for him to stay for two weeks until they can take him. Lucas has been hanging around with a group of older kids that have been involved in breaking and entering and muggings. Susan explains that Lucas is in danger of getting into crime if she does not find a good temporary home for him until the place at the group home becomes available. Susan manages to persuade Ruby to look after Lucas.

When Lucas arrives he spends nearly all of his time on his computer game and hates being stuck away miles from anywhere. He manages to damage the leg of a frog and is horrified when Ruby puts it out of its misery by bashing it to death with a rock. Lucas begins to realise the harm he has done to another living creature and Ruby makes it clear that she will not tolerate this behaviour. Lucas becomes interested in a pair of nesting Loons that have laid an egg early in the season and is keen to see it the egg hatch. Lucas begins to show the sensitive side of his nature when he recognises how much Ruby must be missing her husband. From this point on, Lucas begins to feel comfortable in Ruby's company.

THE SCENE IN CONTEXT

The extract begins about half way through the play and goes through to the end.

Loon Boy

By

Kathleen McDonnell – Canada (1993)

CAST LIST

Lucas – age eleven
Ruby – a foster mother, mid-fifties or older
Susan – a social worker
Puppet Manipulators, for bird puppets, depict two adult loons, male and female, and a baby loon, as well as an eagle.

Setting

The playing space consists of areas representing the inside and outside of Ruby's cottage on a Northern Ontario lake. Also on the lake is the rock with several Native pictographs (rock drawings), where Ruby's loon nest-island will be anchored.

Scene One

*Evening. In the house. **Ruby** cleans up from supper while **Lucas** plays his computer game.*

Ruby Almost time to get ready for bed, Lucas.

Lucas Not yet. I just started Level Five. It's really cool.

Ruby *looking over his shoulder* Just what is it you kids see in these things, anyway?

Lucas See this little guy here? I'm playing him, and this mean ugly monster ZAR keeps trying to kill me, so I have to get past him and each time I do, I get to another level. But it keeps getting harder and harder to get by ZAR. There, that's one of his creepy little gnomes. You gotta kill it, see?

Ruby It's awfully violent.

Lucas That's the fun of it. Anyway, they're bad guys. It's okay to kill bad guys. Oops! Missed one!

Ruby What's that noise mean?

Lucas Just that I have to go back to the start of Level Five again. Here, you try.

Ruby Me? Nooo. I'm useless around computers.

Lucas It's easy. I'll take it back to Level One.

Ruby It's getting late, Lucas…

Lucas Come on, just try it. To start the action you press this. Then you move the little guy along like this. See?

Ruby *taking the game* All right. Just for a minute…

Lucas Okay, now keep moving him along. There, there, get that weapon! No, no. You're letting it get away! Rats! Keep going, you can try for the next one. Wait! There's another one of those gnomes. You gotta go around him, you don't have a weapon, you… A h h h h!

Ruby What happened?

Lucas You're dead.

Ruby I'm dead? That's what happens when you lose? You die?

Lucas Sure. Either you kill them first or they kill you. That's the way it works.

Ruby Well, so much for my computer game career. Now get ready for bed.

Lucas Sorry. I guess I shouldn't have said that.

Ruby Said what?

Lucas About … being dead. I didn't mean to remind you, or anything.

116

91

Ruby Remind me? Oh, you mean about Alf? It's all right, Lucas. I know you didn't mean anything by it.

Lucas Will I still be here when that egg hatches?

Ruby Hmm. Let's see. It'll probably be another three weeks, but Susan did say a month or so. Why? Would you like to be here?

Lucas Yeah. Yeah, I really would.

Ruby I don't see why not. I'll call Susan tomorrow and let her know. That way you can be the first to see the chick swimming around on the mother's back. Now, go to bed.

Lucas I still think she's a lousy mother. Leaving her nest like that.

Ruby You're still rather bothered by that, aren't you?

Lucas She should stay and protect it. That's what mothers are supposed to do.

Ruby What about your own mother, Lucas?

Lucas What about her?

Ruby Do you think about her? *(**Lucas** shakes his head)* If you ever want to talk about her…

Lucas What's to talk about? I never see her. She could be dead for all I care.

Ruby Lucas…

Lucas I want to go to sleep now. *(he turns away from her and rolls over)*

Scene Two

*The next day. **Ruby** is showing **Lucas** how to use a pair of binoculars.*

Ruby Now, to focus, just turn this knob here. Slowly, slowly, till everything becomes nice and sharp. Are things getting clearer?

Lucas Yeah. Hey, neat. I can see the mother loon, like she was right up close. She's swimming around right near the nest. Hey, she just dove under.

RUBY Probably trying to catch a fish for lunch. Look up and down the far shore a bit. See what else catches your eye.

LUCAS What's that big opening in the woods over there?

RUBY An old logging road. Years ago they cut a path through the woods so they could haul lumber out. It's pretty overgrown now, but it goes right out to the highway. I walked all the way into town once along that road. Took me five hours.

LUCAS You walked for five hours? Whoa!

RUBY People have been known to do such things and survive, Lucas. Look! Over there. Check out that bird. See if you can catch it in the binoculars. Use the focus knob the way I showed you.

LUCAS Got it.

RUBY What's it like?

LUCAS Big. Kinda brownish.

RUBY Hmm. Could be an eagle. Got to watch those guys. They're nest-raiders.

LUCAS It's starting to circle over near the nest. And I don't see the mother anywhere.

RUBY Keep an eye on it, Lucas. I'll be right back. I thought I heard a car motor.

*Lucas moves closer to the nest-island, still absorbed in looking through the binoculars. **Susan** enters but he doesn't see her. During **Ruby** and **Susan**'s exchange, an eagle appears and swoops down near the nest-island a few times, as **Lucas** watches fearfully.*

RUBY Susan!

SUSAN Surprise! She strikes without warning again.

RUBY You must've read my mind. I tried to call you this morning, but they said you'd be out for the day.

SUSAN Well, I've got news for you and I just had to deliver it in person. I got a call from the group home this morning and guess what? A space has come up for Lucas. Somebody moved out earlier than expected.

RUBY Oh.

SUSAN He can move in right away. Isn't that great?

RUBY You mean, you want to take him there right now?

SUSAN Oh, no rush. You can take your time getting his things together and I'll finally get that cup of coffee you owe me.

RUBY Well, I'm … flabbergasted.

SUSAN Told you I'd take him off your hands soon as I could. Ruby, what's the matter? I thought you'd be glad.

RUBY Something's come up. That's why I tried to get hold of you this morning.

SUSAN What?

LUCAS *to the eagle* Hey!

116 **RUBY** Lucas has gotten very attached to the loons. He's all excited about the nest, and last night he asked me if he could stay here till the egg hatches.

SUSAN When will that be?

RUBY Another three weeks.

SUSAN Three weeks? I can't leave him here that long, Ruby. They won't hold the space.

LUCAS *to the eagle* Beat it!

RUBY You told me I'd have him six weeks. That's why I told him he could stay to see the chick. I didn't think there'd be any problem.

SUSAN I'm sorry, Ruby. How could I know a space would come up this soon?

RUBY Look, I know this loon thing doesn't sound like a big deal, but it is to Lucas. It's like he's finally found a way to connect with something outside himself, and I want to see it through with him.

SUSAN I see what you're saying, Ruby, but I don't know what I can do. This group home has kids clamouring to get in. If we don't take the space some other agency will snatch it up, and we'll be right back at square one.

RUBY That kid gets shunted around like a piece of furniture.

LUCAS *to the eagle* Go on, beat it.

SUSAN You think I enjoy this? Trying to find homes for kids absolutely nobody wants? You of all people should know what I'm up against.

RUBY I'm sorry.

SUSAN Look, the group home's not that far from here. I can try to swing it so he can come back for a visit when the egg hatches.

RUBY Right. The group home staff are really going to have time to go driving Lucas around the countryside.

SUSAN I'll bring him myself if I have to. It's the best I can do, Ruby.

LUCAS *making shooting motions at the eagle* Kapow! Kapow!

RUBY Listen, he hasn't noticed you're here. I want you to go now and come back tomorrow.

SUSAN Tomorrow? Ruby, I drove all the way up here...

RUBY I need time to break it to him. If you slip up the driveway now he won't see you.

SUSAN Ruby, I ...

LUCAS *to the eagle* You're history, scumbag! Kapow!

RUBY Let me handle this my way, Susan. If that boy's well-being means anything, you can wait one more day.

SUSAN All right. I really am sorry about this.

RUBY I know. *(the eagle flies away)*

SUSAN I'll see you tomorrow around noon.

RUBY Fine. Good-bye, Susan. *(**Susan** exits. **Lucas** rushes back to **Ruby**)*

LUCAS Mrs Laughlin! You were right! It was an eagle and it … Hey, that looks like Mrs Petrillo's car up at the end of the driveway. Wha…? She's pulling away.

RUBY Oh, she was just checking in.

LUCAS Funny she didn't talk to me. They usually do. 'How do you like your placement, Lucas?' As if they cared.

RUBY She was in a bit of a hurry to get back to the city.

LUCAS It was just like you said! The eagle was after the egg! It came swooping down really low over the nest, and the mother swam away. But I scared it off! Really, I did! It flew away!

RUBY Good work, Lucas.

LUCAS I bet it thought I was a hunter. *(pretending to shoot)* Kapow! Kapow! *(he races down to the shore again, as **Ruby** watches)*

Scene Three

*That night. **Ruby** and Lucas in the house. **Lucas** is playing his ZAR game as usual.*

LUCAS In this level, ZAR keeps popping new arms every time I shoot one off. Rats! Did it again! I swear I'll never get past this one.

RUBY You'll have to finish up soon, Lucas.

LUCAS You haven't complained about the noise once tonight. How come?

RUBY Guess my mind's been somewhere else. Lucas, there's something we need to talk about. Mrs Petrillo … had some news for me today.

LUCAS Yeah? What?

RUBY A space has come up for you in the group home, Lucas.

LUCAS Oh?

RUBY Mrs Petrillo just got the call this morning. Someone moved out earlier than expected. So it looks like you'll finally be able to settle down in one place for a while. Mrs Petrillo is thrilled. She thinks it's a really good place.

Lucas Yeah, they always say that. When do I go?

Ruby Tomorrow. But I'm going to arrange for you to…

Lucas Tomorrow?

Ruby I told her all about the egg, Lucas. She knows how important it is for you to be here, and she promised she'd arrange for you to come back and visit around that time.

Lucas Visit? You said I could stay!

Ruby I know I did, Lucas. I didn't think there'd be any problem. Neither Mrs Petrillo nor I had any idea a space would come open this soon.

Lucas But you said!

Ruby Honey, if it were up to me, I'd …

Lucas I thought you were different but you're just like all the others.

Ruby Lucas, listen to me …

Lucas You do it for the money, just like everybody else. You're probably ticked off they're taking me early so you won't make as much!

Ruby That's not true, Lucas …

Lucas *running out of the house* I'm just as glad anyway. This place sucks. It's boring. I hate it!

Ruby Lucas, come back here! (***Lucas*** *races over to the canoe, gets in and pushes off with the paddle before she can reach it*) Lucas, what do you think you're doing? (***Lucas*** *paddles away quickly.* ***Ruby*** *races along the shore, unable to stop him*) Lucas! Get back here this minute! It's getting dark! Lucas!

Lucas I'll get you. I'll show you. (*he arrives at the nest-island and practically slams the canoe right into it. The mother loon, fearful, slides off the nest and swims away, giving a tremulous distress call. He pokes* *the egg with the paddle)* See? I can do anything I want to it! You can't stop me! Aren't you going to do something? Aren't you gonna protect it? Huh? Stupid bird! *(he slams the paddle down on the egg. A loud crack!)* Who cares? Stupid bird.

RUBY *her voice is heard in the distance* Lucas! Lucas! *(**Lucas** paddles to the far shore near the nest-island and gets out of the canoe)*

LUCAS I'll find that road she was talking about. When it gets light. I'll hitch a ride to Toronto and see if I can find my buddies. Too dark now. She can't come after me. She's got no motor. Yeah. I'll find that road. Five hours. She's an old bag, take me half that time. Man, it's dark. I can't even see the house anymore. Why can't I see her light? Getting cold.

He holds himself, starting to shiver. After a few moments he lies down on the ground and curls up in a fetal position. Lights fade to black.

Scene Four

*Lucas' dream-journey begins. The actions in this sequence can be carried out by the bird puppets, possibly in combination with shadow-images on a rear screen. The soundscape and lighting should make clear that everything is occurring in dream-time, not ordinary reality. **Lucas** appears to wake up. He gets up, a bit groggy, and looks around.*

LUCAS Hey, where am I …? Oh, yeah. Yeah. The egg. Oh man, she's gonna kill me when she finds out … *(he suddenly spies the loon egg in the nest. Miraculously, it is whole again, undamaged, looking, if anything, larger and more perfect than before)* Whoa man! I don't believe it! I could have sworn I … *(**Ruby** suddenly appears. She seems to be carrying something behind her back. She glares at **Lucas**)* Ruby? Oh, wow, am I ever glad to see you! I was really…

RUBY How would you like it if somebody hurt you for no reason? How would it make you feel?

LUCAS Huh? *(**Ruby** walks past him toward the egg. She pulls out the object from her back – a rock – and lifts it over her head)* Ruby? Ruby! *(rushing toward her)* What are you doing?

RUBY Finishing what you started.

LUCAS No, you can't do that!

RUBY This is quicker and kinder, believe me. (*Lucas manages to stop her just in time. They struggle over the rock. He finally manages to wrest it from her*)

LUCAS What is it with you? (*Ruby suddenly starts to giggle*)

RUBY Oh, come on. It's just a game.

LUCAS Yeah? You had me scared for a minute there.

RUBY You know that game. It's called: Kill them before they kill you! (*she starts to laugh uproariously*) It's fun!

LUCAS You are completely insane! (*Ruby exits, still laughing. Lucas hears a small cracking sound behind him and whirls around*) What's that? (*he watches in awe as small cracks begin to appear in the egg*) Wow. That's wicked! (*more and more cracks appear, until the sides of the egg fall away, revealing a loon chick. The chick fluffs up its down*) Hey, little guy. Hey. (*the loon mother appears. The loon chick slides onto her back, and they start swimming around*) That is so cool! It's just like she said. (*the mother loon dives for a fish. She brings it up to the surface and feeds it to the loon chick*) Wow. You got quite an appetite, little guy. (*the mother loon begins flapping her wings along the surface of the water, preparing to take off. The loon chick flaps its wings in imitation*) See? She's trying to teach you to fly, little guy. That's right. Keep working at it. You'll get it. (*the mother loon takes off and flies away*) Hey! Where you going? Wait up! You can't just leave him here! He's too little. He doesn't know how to fly yet! (*to the chick*) Don't worry, little guy. She probably just went to a lake where there's better fishing. I bet your dad's on his way right now. Loon fathers do that, you know. They help take care of the babies… (*an eagle appears in the sky overhead*) Uh-oh. (*the eagle begins to swoop down toward the loon chick, who manages to dive under the water to escape*) He can't stay down that long. I don't know what to do. I gotta get some help! (*the loon chick surfaces. The eagle makes another terrifying swoop toward it as it dives under the surface again*) Oh no. No. Somebody! Help! Help! (*Lucas begins to run, screaming. He sees a woman standing with her back to him. He calls to her*) Mom? Mommy? Is that you? You gotta help me,

Mom. That eagles's after the loon chick and … *(the woman turns around and faces **Lucas**. It's **Susan**.)* Oh, it's you. Sorry, Mrs Petrillo, I …

SUSAN You think I enjoy this? Trying to find a home for a kid nobody wants?

LUCAS Please, Mrs Petrillo! You gotta help me! I gotta save the baby loon! Please…

SUSAN *walking away, ignoring him* What can I do about it? There's too many messed-up kids and not enough places to put them. Just too many messed-up kids. *(**Susan** exits. **Lucas** races back and starts attacking the eagle with imaginary weapons)*

LUCAS You're history, scumbag! *(finally the eagle flies away)* He's gone. We did it. We're okay, little guy. See? We showed him. We're okay. We can do it. I'll take care of you little guy. I won't leave you. *(after a moment, the eagle returns. **Lucas** clutches the baby loon protectively)* It's okay, little guy. Don't worry. I won't let him get you. *(the eagle dive-bombs the two of them again. There is a struggle. **Lucas** fights hard but the eagle snatches the baby loon away from him and takes off again. **Lucas** tries to chase after the eagle)* No! No! *(**Ruby** enters carrying something)* Ruby! Ruby, you gotta help me! An eagle came and … *(he stops suddenly, realising she is holding the baby loon)*

116 **RUBY** If somebody bigger and stronger comes after you, there's not a whole lot you can do about it. *(she hands **Lucas** the baby loon. It falls limp in his arms.)*

LUCAS *sobbing* No! No!

End of Dream Sequence.

Scene Five

*Lucas suddenly wakes up to find **Ruby** standing over him.*

LUCAS Ruby!

116 **RUBY** Lucas! Thank god.

Lucas Man, am I glad to see you.

Ruby You scared the living daylights out of me!

Lucas How'd you get here?

Ruby I figured you might head for that old logging road, so I drove to the highway and hiked in. Why did you do this, Lucas?

Lucas I don't know. I'm sorry.

Ruby Come on. We'll talk about it back at the house. I'll get a neighbour to drive me out to the car later. Where's the paddle? *(spying it)* Oh. *(she walks over to get the paddle and notices the nest)* Oh my God! What happened? Oh, it's all … Look, Lucas, the egg! It's… Oh no! *(she is momentarily overcome with tears)* What could have done this? I just don't understand it. I've never seen a raven tear up an egg like this… Was it like this last night, Lucas?

Lucas I don't know. I didn't look. *(Ruby notices something on the paddle)*

Ruby What's this, Lucas?

Lucas What?

Ruby Why is there blood on this paddle?

Lucas I don't know.

Ruby What happened here, Lucas? Who did that to the egg?

Lucas I said I don't know!

Ruby I want the truth, Lucas! Who did this? Who did this?

Lucas It was an accident…

Ruby You little … *(she raises her hand to hit him, but stops herself)* You wanted to hurt me? You wanted to get back at me? Well, you sure found the way to do it. Mrs Petrillo's coming for you today and you know what? I'm glad. That's it. I'm fed up. I wash my hands of you. *(she turns away from him and heads for the boat)*

Lucas I said it was an accident! If you just give me a chance to explain… *(he runs after her and tries to grab her arm. She shakes him off violently)*

116

RUBY You are one sick boy, Lucas. You're so twisted up inside, they should lock you up and throw away the key right now!

LUCAS I'm sorry! *(calling after her)* I said I'm sorry!

Scene six

Some weeks later. **Susan** *and* **Lucas** *arrive at* **Ruby***'s. As they approach the house* **Lucas** *stops, hangs back.*

SUSAN Lucas? Is something wrong?

LUCAS She hates me. She's gonna kill me.

SUSAN No, she's not.

LUCAS She's gonna chew me out. That's what all this is for, isn't it?

SUSAN Look, Lucas. Ruby wouldn't have had me drive all the way up here just so she could yell at you.

LUCAS Then why?

SUSAN I don't know. Honestly. She said there was something really important she wanted to show you. That's all I know.

LUCAS You're sure she wants to see me?

SUSAN I'm sure. Now, come on. It's going to be okay. *(**Ruby** appears, goes to greet them)*

RUBY Hello there.

SUSAN Hey, what gives? You told me that road would dry up like a bone once summer came. It's muddy as ever!

RUBY Oh, you just need better tires on that thing. Hello, Lucas.

LUCAS Hi.

RUBY How've you been?

LUCAS Okay.

RUBY How's it going at the group home?

Lucas Okay.

Susan They tell me he's turned into quite the gardener. He got put in charge of the tomato patch.

Lucas Yeah. That's what they do there. Gardening and stuff. They even got compost, like you.

Ruby You don't say.

Susan Well, I'll let you two visit for a while. Lucas, I'll pick you up in an hour or so, okay?

Lucas Yeah, sure.

Ruby And there'll be coffee ready by then.

Susan Great. You're on. *(**Susan** exits. Left alone, both **Ruby** and **Lucas** are awkward, a bit nervous)*

Ruby So. Still playing your computer game?

Lucas Nah. I got tired of it.

Ruby Oh, really?

Lucas Yeah, battery ran down one day and I just didn't bother getting another one.

Ruby Dead battery, eh?

Lucas Yeah. *(they both smile at the memory of an earlier fight over a dead battery)*

Ruby Lucas, I owe you an apology.

Lucas Apology? What for? I'm the one who should be sorry.

Ruby No matter what you did, I had no right to say the things I said to you. I was very angry, and very hurt. I'm sorry.

117

Lucas I think about it all the time, Ruby. I still don't know why I did it.

Ruby It's all right, Lucas.

Lucas You hate me, don't you?

RUBY No. (**Ruby** puts her arms around **Lucas** and he begins to cry)

LUCAS I swear I'd give anything if I could bring it back.

RUBY Let's go out in the canoe, Lucas. There's something I want you to see. (**Lucas** wipes his eyes on his shirt and follows her into the canoe. They paddle to the nest island)

LUCAS Look, Ruby! (one of the loons is swimming with a baby on its back)

RUBY It just hatched yesterday.

LUCAS But how …? It couldn't have … I don't get it.

RUBY The mother laid a second egg. When loons lose an egg early in the season, they usually try again. This time we got lucky. That nest-island worked like a charm.

LUCAS Awesome!

109 **RUBY** See, Lucas? Nature doesn't hold grudges. No matter what we do, she just keeps giving us another chance. (the baby loon slides off his mother's back)

LUCAS Look! He's doin' it! He's swimming on his own.

RUBY And look who else is coming. (the father loon appears and does a joyous display overhead. The mother loon flaps her wings, preparing to take off. The baby loon imitates her)

LUCAS Go on, little guy. You can do it. (the mother loon takes off. The baby loon flaps harder, on the verge of lifting off) That's it. Yes! Keep it up! You're doing it. (finally the baby loon takes off) Way to go, little guy!

The End

Staging the extract

SET DESIGN

The setting for the play is quite complicated as it involves interior and exterior scenes and a journey across a lake. The play is written specifically for a young audience, so it is important that the setting and the space for the drama capture the imagination of young people. Rather than staging the play on a theatre stage, think about creating the theatre space in a primary school hall. This means that you can forget about sitting the audience on chairs and have the children sitting on the floor. In this way, the audience of children can become the lake and the actors can move through them.

Read through the extract, making a note of the different locations and any props and puppets that you will need.

This is a possible layout for the play.

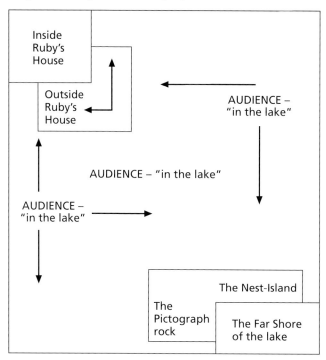

◆4a Setting

The stage layout suggested in the diagram requires the use of a large hall space and uses a variation on traverse staging where the action goes across the audience. Consider other ways of staging the play. How would you stage the extract with the audience "end-on" or "in-the-round"? Remember that the action of the play needs to flow freely from one scene to another without long pauses in between to change scenery. Draw a ground plan showing the layout of your set and present your ideas to the rest of the class.

The one piece of scenery suggested in the script is a rock with several pictograph drawings on it done by North American Indians. Research and present a carefully selected range of North American Pictograph drawings and discuss which ones you are going to use in your final design and why.

PROPERTIES

Most of the properties are straightforward to acquire, but the canoe and paddle, the nest-island and the loon's egg are very specific properties and need to be carefully researched.

This is a description of a Nest-island built by some Boy Scouts near Lake Michigan:

> The island platform we built was a square 4½ feet by 4½ feet using 4" PVC pipe as the frame, black nylon webbing and 1 gallon plastic containers for additional floatation. The frame is strong and provides some flotation. The plastic containers were attached using cable ties until the right amount of buoyancy was achieved. When the basic platform is completed and an island is taken to its location, the top is covered with cattails and other plant material taken from the shoreline. The island is then anchored in place with cement blocks tied with rope to the platform.

◆4b

What impression does this give you of a nest-island? The one in the play has to be lightweight because Ruby has to carry it on stage in an earlier scene and she takes Lucas out in the canoe with it to float it in the water. Draw up your own plans for a nest-island, obtain the materials for it and construct it.

Discuss how you might construct the "dream sequence egg". How are you going to make cracks appear in it? How is it going to open so that the loon chick puppet can emerge from inside?

PUPPETS

One of the features of *Loon Boy* is its use of puppets to represent the birds in the play. The extract requires male and female Loon puppets, a Loon chick puppet and an Eagle puppet. Each puppet will require a manipulator to operate it. The most appropriate type of puppets for this play is likely to be *rod puppets*, which can be held up in the air and moved around freely. The Loon Puppets could be made so that they sit on an actor's head with the head and neck operated by rods or wires by the actor underneath.

The Loon is an important character in the play and you will need to study how it looks and moves.

A common loon on its nest.

4d Movement

There is a sequence in the play where an Eagle is threatening the Loons. You will need to observe the way in which an eagle and a loon moves if you are going to ensure that the movement of the puppets you make resembles that of the real birds. You can then choreograph the movement of the birds rather like a dance.

LIGHTING

Lighting can be used to focus on the different locations in the play and to emphasise the interior and exterior scenes. Special effects like moving water projections or ripple projectors can be used to create the effect of light being reflected off the water of the lake. There is scope for the use of some inventive lighting in the dream-sequence (Scene 4) to create a sense of unreality.

 COSTUMES

The play can be set at almost any time in the last 20 years. The clothes are relatively straightforward to obtain as the fashions and styles worn in Canada and North America are very similar to those worn in the United Kingdom. The costumes need to reflect the age differences of the characters and suit the personalities of each of the characters.

SOUND

There are three important elements to the sound in this extract:

1. The electronic soundscape associated with Lucas's computer game

2. The exterior sounds of wildlife, particularly the call of the loons and the cry of the eagle

3. The sound world of Lucas's dream journey.

The electronic game sound effects can be created as original effects using sound samples and synthesised sounds or you may just be able to record the sounds made by an existing computerised game.

The sounds made by the Loon are very distinctive and you will need to research wildlife sound recordings to obtain the particular cry of the loon you require.

The use of sound in the dream sequence can be effective in creating a sense of a different world from the other scenes in the play. In a group discuss the different ways that you might use sound to create the right effect.

Exploring the extract

GENRE AND SUBJECT MATTER

Loon Boy is written as a piece of Children's Theatre or Theatre for Young Audience as it is called in Canada. The purpose of the play is to enable an audience of children around the age of 11 years old to empathise with the attitudes and behaviour of Lucas who is unable to live with his parents. At the beginning of the play, Susan fills Ruby in on Lucas's background.

SUSAN Oh, you've heard it all before. Doesn't know his father. Mother lives in Kirkland Lake. She was only sixteen when she had him … She had this boyfriend. Real sweetheart of a guy. When Lucas was four, they brought him into Sick Kids with a broken shoulder and bruises over half his body. Tried to tell the doctors he had a fall. Typical. The cops knew it was the boyfriend but they couldn't get the mother to testify against him … We took Lucas into care and found a family to adopt him. But it just didn't work out. He's been in and out of foster homes ever since.

On one level the play is a social drama but on another it is an allegory or fable about the significance of the relationship between parents and their children. The way in which the loons bring up their young is used as a comparison to the way in which Lucas has been brought up by his mother. Again, researching this issue as a group will help you to understand how the author is using the comparison.

◆4d Second chances

At the end of the play, Ruby says to Lucas, "See, Lucas? Nature doesn't hold grudges. No matter what we do, she just keeps giving us another chance."

In your opinion, does Lucas deserve another chance after smashing the Loon egg? Why does Ruby forgive him? What sort of an ending does the play have? What do you think might happen next after the last line of the play is spoken?

104

◆4e Drama techniques: Cross-cutting

The events in *Loon Boy* happen over a period of weeks and the plot is told in the order that the events happen in real time. The **cross–cutting** technique can be used to show the relationship between scenes 2 and 3 of the extract and how what is said in scene 2 affects what happens and what is said in scene 3.

In groups

Divide your performance space into two separate areas: scene 2 happens on one side of the stage and scene 3 happens on the other side of the stage. (It is even more effective if you can use lighting so that you can cross fade from one side of the stage to the other.)

Two actors are cast as Ruby and Lucas in Scene 2 and two different actors are cast as Ruby and Susan for Scene 3. Scene 2 and Scene 3 are seen happening at the same time on stage but the action and dialogue cuts back and forward between the two scenes.

Rehearse the **cross–cut** version of scenes 2 and 3 that follows and perform them to an audience. What does this exercise tell you about the different reactions to Susan's news? What does the exercise tell you about Ruby's character?

Scene 2	Scene 3
RUBY Lucas, there's something we need to talk about. Mrs Petrillo … had some news for me today.	
	SUSAN Well, I've got news for you and I just had to deliver it in person. I got a call from the group home this morning and guess what?
RUBY A space has come up for you in the group home, Lucas.	
	RUBY Something's come up. He's all excited about the nest, and last night he asked me if he could stay here till the egg hatches.

Scene 2	Scene 3
Ruby I told her all about the egg, Lucas. She knows how important it is for you to be here, and she promised she'd arrange for you to come back and visit around that time. **Lucas** Visit? You said I could stay!	
	Ruby You told me I'd have him six weeks. That's why I told him he could stay to see the chick. I didn't think there'd be any problem. **Susan** I'm sorry, Ruby. How could I know a space would come up this soon?
Lucas I thought you were different but you're just like all the others. **Ruby** Lucas, listen to me …	
	Ruby That kid gets shunted around like a piece of furniture. **Susan** You think I enjoy this? Trying to find homes for kids absolutely nobody wants? You of all people should know what I'm up against. **Ruby** I'm sorry.
Lucas You do it for the money, just like everybody else. You're probably ticked off they're taking me early so you won't make as much! **Ruby** That's not true, Lucas…	
	Ruby Let me handle this my way, Susan. If that boy's well-being means anything, you can wait one more day. **Susan** All right. I really am sorry about this. **Ruby** I know.

Scene 2	Scene 3
Lucas *Running out of the house* This place sucks. It's boring. I hate it! **Ruby** Lucas, come back here! (*Lucas races over to the canoe, gets in and pushes off with the paddle before she can reach it.*) Lucas, what do you think you're doing? (*Lucas paddles away quickly. Ruby races along the shore, unable to stop him.*) Lucas! Get back here this minute! It's getting dark! Lucas! **Lucas** I'll get you. I'll show you.	

◆4f Cross-cutting 2

In groups

Create your own **cross–cut** version of scenes 5 and 6 in the same way as with Scenes 2 and 3; rehearse it and perform it to your class. Discuss with the rest of your class what the exercise shows you about the content and the characters in the play.

Exploring characters

SUSAN

Susan is a social worker and it would be easy to portray her as a stereotype. However, it is important to recognise that Susan has gone to a lot of trouble to persuade Ruby to come out of retirement and to look after Lucas for a while to get him away from trouble. Susan has a line earlier in the play when she says, "I promised my kids I'd be home for supper", which shows that not only is she a social worker but that she is a mother herself too.

◆4g Role-play

In threes

Organisation: You will need the following roles: Susan – Lucas's Social Worker; John or Jane – The Group Home Manager, and Eileen or Edward – Head of the Social Services Department.

Situation: The Case Meeting at the Social Services Department to discuss Lucas's future. The meeting decides to place Lucas in the Group Home, however, there are the following problems that need to be resolved during the meeting:

a There are no places in the Group Home for at least six weeks

b There are two other children who are next on the list to be offered places at the Group Home

c The Head of Social Services is concerned about the cost of placing Lucas in the Group Home. Lucas will be a long way from the city and his mother may want to visit him, this means they will have to pay for her transport.

Develop this role-play, so that Susan's proposal to put Lucas with Ruby on a temporary basis is accepted.

How does this exercise help develop the character of Susan? What does it tell you about the sort of person Susan is?

◆4h **The phone call**

Between Scenes 5 and 6, there is a gap of some weeks. During that time, Ruby has phoned Susan to persuade her to bring Lucas back to the lake to see the newly hatched baby loon. She just tells Susan that she wants to surprise Lucas. Write or improvise the dialogue for the phone conversation between Ruby and Susan.

LUCAS

One of the things that characterises Lucas in the play is the changes in mood and attitude he goes through. At one moment he is positive about things. For example,

RUBY Would you like to be here?

LUCAS Yeah. Yeah, I really would.

At other times he becomes almost the opposite in his attitude:

LUCAS This place sucks. It's boring.

◆4i **Characterisation**

Draw two columns on a piece of paper and write "Lucas's Good Moods" at the top of one column and "Lucas's Bad Moods" at the top of the other column. Go through the extract and find examples of each for the chart.

In groups

Working in two groups present the two sides of Lucas in the play. Group A share performing at least five relevant episodes of Lucas in a Good Mood, and Group B performing at least five episodes of Lucas in a Bad Mood. Each group watches the other group's presentation so that you are seeing the opposite mood of Lucas to the one you have been acting.

cont...

Discuss the ways in which each group portrays Lucas. What is different about vocal expression, facial expressions and the use of gesture and posture? What is it that makes Lucas behave in these extreme ways?

♦4j Narration

H

You are going to add a **Narrator** character to the play. The Narrator is Lucas as an adult in his late 20s looking back at his life when he was 11 years old. Here is an imaginary narration that goes at the start of Scene 1.

NARRATOR *(to the audience)* This was me when I was 11. I was a right tearaway then. I got fostered out to this old lady. Ruby Laughlin her name was. That's why I've come back to this place. To the lakeside. To remember Ruby now that she's gone and the kindness she did me back then. I'll miss her. *(The sound of a loon is heard)* Do you hear that? The cry of a loon calling its mate. That's what brought Ruby and me close together. It all started when Social Services decided they need to put me out of harm's way for a while…

Write your own narration for the beginning of Scenes 2, 3 and 6.

♦4k Discussion

98–100

What is the purpose of the Dream Sequence (Scene 4) in the play? What does it tell you about Lucas as a character that the other scenes in the play do not reveal?

To what extent do you have any sympathy for Lucas?

In what ways is Lucas a different boy in Scene 6 compared with the way he is earlier in the play?

RUBY

◆4l Hot-seating

Ruby goes through a range of different emotions and it is important for any actor playing the part to explore her range of feelings. One person in the group assumes the role of Ruby and sits in the 'hot-seat'. This person has to answer questions asked by the rest of group from Ruby's point of view. These are the sort of questions you might ask Ruby.

1. What is it you miss most about your husband, Alf?
2. Do you have any regrets about letting Lucas stay with you?
3. What is your opinion of Lucas's mother?
4. Why were you so harsh on Susan when she wanted to take Lucas back earlier than expected?
5. What made you forgive Lucas for smashing the Loon's egg?

◆4m Still image/Marking the moment/Thought-tracking

In groups

This exercise combines a number of drama techniques in order to focus on key points in Ruby's role throughout the extract.

Create a still image of each of the following episodes in the extract:

1. Lucas thinks he's reminded Ruby about her dead husband, Alf
2. Ruby asks Lucas about his mother
3. Ruby explains to Susan how important the loons have become to Lucas
4. Ruby calls out after Lucas who has run out into the night
5. Ruby presents Lucas with the dead baby loon
6. Ruby finds Lucas who awakes from his dream
7. Ruby goes to hit Lucas for smashing the egg

8. Ruby apologises to Lucas for the things she said

■ Mark the moment by speaking the still image caption as a chorus
■ Speak the thoughts of Ruby in each still image
■ Speak the thoughts that the other characters in each still image have about Ruby

◆4n **Writing**

Imagine that it is 10 years on from when the events in the play happened. Ruby has finally retired but she is still living by the lake. Write a monologue for Ruby that tells the story of the spring and summer she spent with a boy called Lucas.

COMPARING TEXTS – SOCIETY AND CULTURE

◆4p Themes for Comparison: Parents, families and marriage

■ In each of the plays in this collection, there is a Mother figure. How is the role of a mother portrayed in each of the plays? What are the similarities and differences between the different representations of the role of a mother?

■ In *Summer of the Aliens* and *Loon Boy*, both Lewis and Lucas come from unstable family backgrounds. Lewis grows up only seeing and knowing his father for two short periods in his life whilst Lucas has never known his father. What effects does this have on the boys in these two plays? What do the plays tell you about the relationship between parents and children?

■ *The Government Inspector* and *Anowa*, both deal with the issues of daughters leaving home to get married. How is the parents' attitude to marriage different in these two plays? Would you expect your own parents to behave like the parents in these two plays?

cont…

- Each of the plays in this collection belongs to a different culture. Describe **one** aspect of each play that identifies it as belonging to its particular culture. It may be in the content of the play, in what happens in the play or in what people say in the play. Share your descriptions in a group discussion and identify unique cultural characteristics for each of the four plays.

Exploring and comparing the four extracts

COMPARING TEXTS – PERIOD, CULTURE AND SOCIETY

◆5a The Places

In groups

Organisation: Work in four small groups. Each group is going to represent the Tourist Board for the four places in the extracts: Group 1 for the small Russian Town of Gogolstrovsky; Group 2 for the suburb of Fawkner, Melbourne, Australia; Group 3 for the village of Aidoo, Ghana, West Africa, and Group 4 for the Laughlin Lake area, Ontario, Canada.

Situation: You are going to create a two minute advertisement that will attract tourists to your particular location. The advertisement will take the form of a guided journey through the landmarks of the particular place you are representing. Make a list of any landmarks or places of interest using information from the play extract as well as additional research material. You can include the characters from the play being interviewed about the place in which they live as well as characters of your own making. You might also select a suitable piece of music to accompany the advertisement. The sequence of events will need to be linked by a voice-over or by a Travel Guide who describes the journey through your location.

Presentation: Each group presents their travelogue advertisement either as a live event or by showing a video recording of the advertisement.

As a class

What do you find most and least attractive about each of the locations and why? What particular features make the place different to any other? Would the events and characters from one play work in one or more of the other locations? If so, which one(s) and how might this change the nature of the play and what it communicates to an audience?

On your own

Write an advertisement for a newspaper highlighting the attractions of your area for visitors. Include a suitable visual image.

◆5b Time machine

The purpose of this activity is to explore the characters from across the extracts through the use of a Time Machine. The exercise is more effective if you have already worked on a particular role from one of the plays.

As a class

Organisation: Individuals assume **ONE** of the following roles with as many of the roles as possible distributed across the whole class: Anowa, Maria, Osam, The Mayor, Eric, Lucas, Young Lewis, Ruby, Anna, Badua or Norma. Each person finds a space in the room and that space becomes a Time Machine. The group leader will touch two or more different characters on the shoulder and this will indicate that their *Time Machine* is activated. These activated characters will come together in a space in the centre of the room and begin an improvisation around a shared issue.

Situation: These are some suggested combinations of characters and a starting point for their improvisation.

Anowa and Maria: What it is like being told what to do by your Mother?
Osam, The Mayor and Eric: Why do wives give their husbands such a hard time?
Lucas and Lewis: Why can't parents stay together?
Ruby and Norma: Would you ever have your child fostered?
Anna and Badua: Getting your daughter to do as she is told.

Evaluation: This exercise literally brings characters together from across different times and cultures. What does it reveal about different character's attitudes that result from their cultural or historical origins? Are there any issues that seem to cross cultural and historical barriers? If so, what are they?

◆5c Making an entrance

In groups

- Identify the moment in each of the extracts when a character or characters enters the scene. Act out each of these moments from the line before the character or characters enters up until 3 or 4 lines after this entrance. Watch or take part in this moment from each of the extracts.

In small groups, discuss the following points:

- How does the interaction between the characters differ between the extracts?

- To what extent is the behaviour and what is being said an indication of any social, cultural or historical differences between the plays?

PARENTS AND CHILDREN

The following activities use two poems as starting points for drama. The poems are linked to the four extracts in that they deal with the relationship between parents and children. Both the poems and the activities are suitable material to use as a resource for devising your own plays.

◆5d Do a Dance for Daddy

In groups

- Read the following poem.

cont...

- Work on a vocal presentation of the poem in groups of 4 to 6. Decide how many voices to put on different lines, phrases or words in the poem. Try out different combinations of voices.

- In the same groups, work out a sequence of movements to accompany the actions in the poem.

- Pair up with another group. Group A of the pair will present their reading of the poem whilst Group B of the pair enacts their movement to it. Group B then presents their reading with Group A performing their accompanying movement. You will need to rehearse the sequences so that the movement and speaking work effectively together.

- Present your performance of the poem to the rest of the class.

As a class

- Discuss what each of the performances reveals about the meaning of the poem. What does it say about the relationship between daughters and their fathers? How does this change as you get older? Can you identify with any of the images in the poem?

Do a Dance for Daddy
by Fran Landesman

Do a dance for Daddy, make your Daddy smile
Be his little angel
Remember you're on trial
Mummy's competition, Mummy brings you down
When you're up there shining
She always wears a frown.

Do a dance for Daddy. Bend and dip and whirl
You've got all that talent
'Cause you're Daddy's girl
Daddy is your hero, witty and superb
With a sign upon his door
That reads, 'DO NOT DISTURB'

Look your best for Daddy
Pass your test for Daddy
Stand up tall for Daddy
Do it all for Daddy

Some day when you're older you will find romance
Someone just like Daddy
Will whistle and you'll dance
You'll recall that music when you're on the shelf
You danced for all the Daddies
But you never found yourself

Paint your eyes for Daddy
Win a prize for Daddy
Swim to France for Daddy
Do your dance for Daddy

◆5e Further activities

The poem is written from the point of view of what a daughter feels her father expects of her. Write your own version of the poem that either expresses either what a son feels his father or mother expects of him or a mother expects of their son or daughter.

Still Images
The poem moves through time. Identify each of the changes of time in the poem and create a still image to represent that moment. Accompany each still image with a spoken section of the poem that describes it.

◆5f Being There

■ Read the following poem carefully.

Being There
by Ethel Portnoy

My child called my name in the street as I rushed past, unseeing.
Later I turned, and saw her stricken face,
The one she'll wear when she is old
When in a dream she'll call my name, and I,
Having joined the dead, rush on –
Not as today, turn back
To clasp her in my arms.

- Why is the poem called *Being There?*
- What emotions does the poem stir up in you?

In pairs

- Person A is in the role of the mother in the poem. Person B is in the role of the daughter in the poem but she is now a teenager. Person A is going to describe in their own words the events that happened in the poem when Person B was very young. Person B must listen carefully and react accordingly.

- As a group, share some of the responses that were given to the story? How did it make people feel?

DEVISED PERFORMANCE

◆5g Putting it together

The opportunity exists within your GCSE course to devise an original piece of drama. It is important when working on a devised piece to think about the structure of your work and to record any ideas that you have as you go along. Remember that a devised piece of theatre needs to communicate to an audience and you should consider the use of different aspects of the medium of drama (e.g. costume, set, lighting, sound etc.) as appropriate.

The following are a list of suggested starting points derived from the extracts in this selection.

- Eric (from *Summer of the Aliens*) turns up in a bar in your town and begins to relate stories about his past. Devise a group of characters around Eric that will begin to make him feel uncomfortable about his past life.

- Anowa's childhood. Create a devised piece showing Anowa at an earlier age when she is interested in dancing and becoming a Priestess. Explore the ways in which her Mother tries to influence her choices in life.

- Create a play for a young audience that uses puppets and masks in a similar way to that used in *Loon Boy*. You could explore themes such as respect for the environment, life as a foster child or the city child being moved to the country.

■ Reread the two poems included above and discuss their potential as a starting point for a piece of devised work. Remember that you can incorporate lines or sections of the poems into your work. What kind of Daddy is the character being written about in the first poem? Could you create this character and a life for him on stage? From the poem, *Being There*, you could start with the moment,

> "When in a dream she'll call my name, and I,
> Having joined the dead, rush on –"

and build a kind of ghost story out of this moment.

COMPARING DRAMATIC TECHNIQUES AND STYLE

◆5h Analysing scripts

This is a list of some of the dramatic conventions and techniques that are used in the plays in this collection:

■ Narration

■ Direct address to the audience

■ Dream sequence

■ Asides

■ Dramatic irony

■ Jump cutting

■ Songs

■ Puppetry

■ Composite setting

Identify where and in which plays each of these are used. What effect do they create in the context in which they are used?

One of the key features of the plays in this collection is that they are set in different countries around the world. On a sheet of paper draw four columns and head each column with the title of the four plays. Under each column list the methods and techniques used by each of the playwrights to ensure that the atmosphere and character of the specific country is captured on stage.

cont...

Examine your completed list and share your findings with others in your class. Are there any striking similarities and/or differences between the methods used by each playwright to locate their play in its unique setting?